W9-AFS-307

Host Family
Survival Kit

HOST FAMILY SURVIVAL KIT
A Guide for American Host Families

By NANCY KING
and KEN HUFF

91-427

INTERCULTURAL PRESS, INC.
Yarmouth, Maine

Library of Congress Catalogue Card Number 83-082533

ISBN 0-933662-52-1

Copyright © 1985 by Nancy King and Ken Huff

First published in 1985 in a paperbound edition
by Intercultural Press, Inc., P.O. Box 768,
Yarmouth, Maine 04096.

Printed in the United States of America

To: Henrique, Carolina, Neilton,
Yuki, Susan, Davy, Mogens, Regina, Christer,
Maria, Caio, Ana, Valerie, Kyoko and Juan.

Their sensitive, introspective, lively and
sometimes puzzling ways deeply impressed us.

Acknowledgments

To the hundreds of exchange students and host families whom we talked to over a period of years, we owe our thanks for the concepts that made this book possible. In addition, a special thanks goes to the following families and individuals who shared their experiences and recommendations: Nanya & Jerry Campbell, Margery Lawson, Verga Mingo, Ray Plato and Bill & Dee Rustic.

Valuable contributions also came from professionals in the fields of student exchange and intercultural and international relations, including: Mary Alvey, Steve Arnold, Diana Follebout, Cornelius Grove, Don Hausrath, Jim Kelman, Bob Kohls, John Kourmadas, Ed Meador, Linda Reed and Ed Silvas. Many of these professionals have participated in programs as either hosts or exchange students.

Among those who read the manuscript and made valuable comments are: Barbara Bost, Alicia Knight, Bev Syvrud, Karen Warns, and LaVerne Yee.

A very special thanks also for the clarifications and additions made by the publisher and editors: Dave Hoopes and Peggy Pusch.

Contents

Foreword

The forty years that have passed since the end of World War II have been unparalleled in the ways they have reduced the autonomy of nations. Communications, transportation, technology, education, commerce and military affairs have become more and more interrelated across national borders. The major issues we face as a nation—unemployment, national security, pollution, immigration, taxes, crime—cannot be addressed solely through domestic action: the resolution of each requires understanding of, and cooperation with, other governments and peoples. This point was very eloquently made in 1980 by the President's Commission on Hunger:

> Demographic, economic, political and environmental world trends have combined in recent years to create a qualitatively different class of unavoidable world-level problems that were virtually unknown to traditional diplomacy; that are beyond the reach of national governments; that cannot be fitted into accepted theories of competitive interstate behavior; that are coming increasingly to dominate world affairs; that cannot be wished away; and that are indifferent to military force.

The implications of these trends are far-reaching. One of the most important is that the world has gone a long way toward integrating itself in terms of "hardware" and technology while values, attitudes and knowledge have generally lagged far behind. Given nuclear weapons, among other things, this gap looms dangerously. The cure for terminal international conflict, total war, is not a viable solution in the nuclear age.

A second significant implication of today's new global situation is that international knowledge and experience can no longer be left to a few highly selected specialists. How we perceive, and vote on, "domestic" issues affects our international relations. How individuals make "private" decisions—how large a family to have, how to dispose of waste, what type of resources to consume—ends up having a major impact on what will be the critical issues of the next generation will be.

It is in this context that youth exchange becomes one of the great educational experiments of our time. Literally hundreds of thousands of young people have in-depth experience in other cultures every year. Since World War II, millions of young people and host family members have shared the challenges and joys of establishing close and meaningful interpersonal relationships across the barriers of language and culture. It is one of the truly inspirational stories of the past forty years that millions of utter strangers have come together, in the most intense of circumstances, with so few really serious problems. The United States is a leader in student exchange, which seems especially suited to our altruism, our commitment to family initiative, our willingness to volunteer for the common good, and our belief in the virtues of an open society. That so many other nations have enthusiastically adopted our idea of youth and student exchange represents an export we can be particularly proud of. It truly represents the best of our values as a people.

Given the significance of youth exchange in preparing young people for their future roles as leaders in an interdependent world, it is remarkable how casually it has been treated. Families spend hundreds of millions of dollars every year to allow their children to live and study in other countries. Tens of thousands of host families dig deep into their hearts and their pocketbooks to add to their household a new young person needing both emotional and financial support. Thousands of schools throughout the world open their classrooms, their sports facilities, and their counseling offices, free of charge, to young people from other countries. Like an immense subterranean river, youth exchange has been quietly carried out by millions of individual students, host family members, and community volunteers, a tribute to what people can do on their own to help themselves and others.

Nevertheless, not all the potential of youth exchange has been achieved, given the large numbers of people involved and the tremendous impact the experience usually has on them. People very often have to stumble through their exchange student/host family experience with no guidance, repeating past mistakes, reinventing the wheel, encountering unnecessary frustrations. Wonderful opportunities for international and intercultural learning are lost through the absence of meaningful frameworks within which to place intense personal feelings. Negative experiences are encountered by highly-motivated families, schools and communities lacking the information to choose between responsible, well-run programs and the increasing number of unethical or inexperienced organizations that are entering the field. Schools and teachers often fail to take full advantage of the educational impact exchange students can have on the foreign language and social studies curriculum, where young people can demonstrate to their peers that these subjects are not just dull abstractions, but relevant and exciting tools for living international communication and understanding.

We are fortunately going through a period of improvement in terms of the availability of materials designed to enrich the youth exchange experience. For example, with grant support from the Youth Exchange Office of the United States Information Agency, the National Association of Foreign Student Affairs has produced a series of monographs to guide secondary school principals on how to take maximum advantage of youth exchange programs. The Experiment in International Living, also with USIA support, has produced a series of self-instructional volumes, dealing with language acquisition and cultural adaptation, for incoming and outbound exchange students, for schoolteachers, and for community volunteers. Not least among this small but important collection of materials on how to get the most out of youth exchange is Nancy King and Ken Huff's *Host Family Survival Kit.*

Bringing a new teenager into one's home for a year, under any set of circumstances, is a challenging, if not intimidating, decision. Add to the basic logistical, emotional and interpersonal stresses and strains the fact that the individual is from another culture, and usually speaks another language, and you have the formula for one of the most intense, stimulating, but also potentially difficult, experiences a family can have. That millions of families around the world have not only survived, but flourished under these circumstances is a tremendous tribute to the creativity, initiative, maturity, and love people can find within them when conditions are right. It is the reaffirmation of these bonds of common humanity, across the barriers of language and culture, that is one of the important contributions of youth exchanges. To quote the slogan of the national advertising campaign of the President's International Youth Exchange Initiative, it "helps brings the world together, one friendship at a time."

Nevertheless, both the promise and the pitfalls of the year-long hosting experience more than justify fully informing oneself about all its ramifications, and *Host Family Survival Kit* meets this need admirably. To begin with, the book suggests criteria for deciding whether or not to become a year-long host family and for selecting a reliable and helpful sponsoring organization. Ten to twenty percent of all long-term exchange experiences do run into problems where outside help is needed, and it is essential that the youth exchange organization is ready, willing and able to respond when the need arises. Without knowing what questions to ask, it is very difficult to know how to assess the ability of the organization to provide help.

The *Host Family Survival Kit* makes its most important contributions, however, in its practical hands-on problem-solving approach to the homestay experience itself. It takes what has been learned over four decades of youth exchange and concentrates it in useful and readable form. It provides a thorough and well-illustrated review of the cross-cultural and psychological dynamics of the experience, and points out the many ways in which good, old-fashioned American common sense might not produce the normally-expected results. It also takes the well-documented psychological cycle of the exchange student year and describes the challenges that are likely to be faced at different points in the year, providing helpful examples of how to deal with each of them. Taken as a whole, it provides a way to greatly enrich the hosting experience, not only as a unique opportunity for personal and family growth, but also as a laboratory for international and intercultural learning.

I can envisage that *Host Family Survival Kit* will not only be read in terms of a basic orientation to the youth exchange year, it will be turned to again and again throughout that year for its helpful insights into specific issues. By making the entire experience more comprehensible, more positive, and more thought-provoking, *Host Family Survival Kit* may well also encourage more families to explore the literature on global issues and international affairs. To that end the book includes a useful starting bibliography on where to go for further background. It may also inspire families to become more involved in the growing movement to increase America's competence in languages and international studies. Both as a guide to a positive hosting experience and as a stimulus to further involvement in international affairs, *Host Family Survival Kit* meets an important need in the international education field.

In the immediate intensity of integrating a foreign teenager into one's home, it is easy to lose sight of the larger purpose that is being achieved. It is a big jump from bathroom scheduling and homesickness to international understanding and global awareness. By pulling together, in a practical way, what the field has learned over the years, Nancy King and Ken Huff have made an important contribution to strengthening the larger purposes of youth exchange. And in a world where international misunderstanding is far more easily prevented than cured, they will help thousands of future host families better carry out their responsibilities as concerned and involved citizens.

Dr. Charles MacCormack, President,
The Experiment in International Living*

---

*The Experiment in International Living (EIL) is the oldest comprehensive international, intercultural education and training organization in the United States. Headquartered in Brattleboro, Vermont, EIL offers a variety of study abroad programs which include extended home stays with families in more than 60 countries.

Authors' Note

We believe that hosting a teenage exchange student can be a highly rewarding and enjoyable cross-cultural experience when families enter it with skills, knowledge and healthy motivations. That is why we have written this book; it reflects our efforts to conceptualize the foreign student's homestay as an intercultural learning experience for American host families.

As perhaps the first attempt to describe the homestay experience from the host's perspective, this effort is merely a beginning point. Other writers will surely augment and revise what is said here.

It is also important to mention that this book is not based on a representative sample which reflects the general population of host families. Rather, it is based on case studies involving selected families who, in our opinion, have been highly effective and successful. These individuals are skilled at helping students adjust to a different lifestyle and culture. They recognize that both the student and the family go through culture shock. And they actively engage in culture learning. Because we have chosen to define the homestay in this way, the content of this book may be more prescriptive than descriptive. In addition, the book is intended to serve as a practical guide rather than an academic study.

In most cases, our use of the phrase "typical hosting experiences"—which we employ throughout the text—is in reference to the special population we have defined. At the same time, we have tried to include what are believed to be some of the common features that most families report.

No cross sectional studies of the hosting experience have yet been published. Except for the theses and dissertations mentioned in the footnotes to this book, there is little hard data available about the "average" or "typical" experience of either students or host families. One such work that has been undertaken is the as yet unpublished "Dynamics of Hosting Study" by Cornelius Grove at

AFS International/Intercultural Programs, which we will refer to a number of times. What we have seen of his study, and what he has told us in personal communications, reveal wide diversity in the course and pattern of individual experiences. However, we feel that neither his study nor any other work with which we are familiar suggests that the basic nature of the experience or the requisites for success are significantly different from what we have found in our own research.

The first six chapters discuss subjects which we consider central to hosting: appropriate roles, lifestyle sharing, the meaning of culture and culture shock, the sojourner's experience, and the host's experience. Part II of the book focuses on practical information that we hope will be especially useful to first-time families. The eight stages that are described represent a composite of experiences reported by numerous host families—none of whom negotiated all of the various phases that we depict, but each provided insight regarding salient features.

Our academic background in developmental psychology undoubtedly influenced our decision to conceptualize the homestay experience in terms of defined stages and tasks which are negotiated in established sequences. However, using such a model introduces a hypothetical element since practical experience rarely follows the elegant precision of theoretical constructs. Nevertheless, we hope that the stages we portray serve as a constructive guide to families.

Introduction: Baseball, Apple Pie, and Pickled Fish in Bottles

What on earth could pickled fish possibly have in common with baseball and apple pie? And what does the combination have to do with hosting a foreign exchange student?

"Pickled fish in bottles" is our way of describing the "foreignness" of foreigners. Beyond the borders of the United States, fish is a delicacy that is savored raw (Japan), bottled in a spicy brine (Scandinavia) or marinated with salted lime and lemon juice (South America). But most people in the United States like fish only when it is thoroughly cooked—better yet when it is fileted, breaded and deep fried.

You know the stage has been set for the melding of two very different cultures when a baseball-loving American[1] family serves its foreign exchange student a juicy, sweet slice of apple pie. The well-meaning student reciprocates by opening up a bottle and offering in return a prized treat of tangy pickled fish with head and eyes fully intact. Being unaccustomed to rich desserts, the student nibbles at the pie, while the family picks courteously at the fish. The result: stomachs from both cultures churn, but the mix of shock and curiosity opens the way for a cross-cultural experience of major proportions—an experience with the potential of being at once hilarious, enriching, tender, frustrating and, at times, heart-rending.

The collision and intertwining of differences is what cross-cultural encounters are all about. It is the intent of this book to explore with you the nature of such encounters and to provide guidelines about how to survive them. But more than just survive, we want to help you reap the rewards that cross-cultural experiences offer. As we spend the next 100 or so pages together, we hope to prepare your spirit—if not your digestive tract—for "pickled fish in bottles" and a thousand other curiosities and calamities that occur when cultures come together.

How did all this get started? Although dozens of international teenage exchange programs exist today, the concept got its start in the aftermath of World War II. At that time, by encouraging NATO alliance youth to take up residence in the United States and by exporting American teenagers to live with European families, the U.S. hoped both to make friends abroad and to increase understanding.

As originally conceived, foreign teenagers would live with an American family in the U.S. for a year and, typically, attend high school. The American family would agree to provide room, board and a generous slice of American life. In return, the teenager would impart knowledge about his or her country, thereby enriching the family with the customs and traditions of distant lands. A program fee would cover airfare, orientation, support services, medical backup and in some cases language training.

While this remains the most common exchange pattern, over the years the original mission—to widen circles of friendship between Americans and Europeans—has been expanded. Teenagers are now being placed in more than sixty countries around the globe each year. Some programs stress the study abroad aspect, requiring high academic credentials and language proficiency. Many programs place primary importance on the personal growth that occurs in the family living experience. Their literature reminds the reader that if it's cultural learning you are seeking, the overseas family is the world's greatest classroom. Other programs appeal to the adolescent's love of high adventure and quest for identity by enticing the student with the challenge: Find yourself in another world.

In addition to the standard type of exchange, there are some newer, hybrid varieties: a domestic exchange student program within the U.S.; an arrangement for placing teenagers in alternative group-living situations such as with archeological projects or on farm collectives; a student ambassador program; short-term summer homestays which may highlight language training, visits to historical sites or participation in art institutes. For one program, U.S. Senators nominate outstanding teenagers for study abroad in Japan, Finland and Germany.

By the early 1980's, hundreds of thousands of young people

had participated in overseas homestay programs, and today, the globe is virtually encircled by exchange organizations which provide a smorgasbord of cross-cultural options. Young people are placed in small towns, sleepy hamlets and bustling metropolitan centers; they take up residence in tongue-twister cities like Reykjavik, Iceland, or exotic Jakarta, Indonesia. Placed on almost every continent, students travel to both northern and southern hemispheres, live with families of Moslem, Shinto, Christian, Jewish or Buddhist religious persuasion—or of no religious persuasion—and are exposed to the political creeds of both developing and highly industrialized nations.

During the summer months when hundreds of students arrive and depart en masse, international airports become friendly mob scenes. And, on a year-round basis, telex messages zipping across continents announce to natural parents: *"Congratulations! Host family found for your daughter,"* or *"Please write to horribly homesick son,"* or *"Student broke! Send money soonest."*

Many American families regularly receive letters and mementos from a number of foreigners who at one time or another shared a year with them. Of the thousands of students who have participated in homestay experiences, some have gone on to become world leaders, mayors and governors, international policymakers and corporate executives for multinational businesses.

The original concept has mushroomed, creating a gigantic network of teenagers, host and natural families, overseas and domestic community volunteers, professionals and dignitaries. As President Reagan said in 1982 when he announced a new initiative to increase international exchanges:

> I am convinced that one of the best ways to develop more accurate perspectives on other nations and on ourselves is for more Americans to join, for a time, a family and a community in another land. And we cannot hope that other nations will appreciate our country unless more of their future leaders have had the same chance to feel the warmth of the American family, the vitality of an American community, [and] the diversity of our educational system.

Host Family
Survival Kit

PART I

An Overview of the Hosting Experience

1. What Exactly
Is an Exchange Student?

Is there a particular role that an exchange student is expected to assume? Is he or she similar to a new family member? A weekend house guest? A neighborhood friend? A cleaning lady? Or what?

People who live together as a family develop a bond of shared experiences, hold common expectations and act more casually than they would at work or in other public places. At home, family members know they can let their hair down and relax. It matters little if someone yawns in the middle of a conversation or neglects to stifle a burp. Likewise, addressing each other by affectionate nicknames (such as Sis or Motormouth) or diminutives (Diana becomes Di) is encouraged.

In some households, family members can run around in a modified version of their birthday suit and no one will bat an eyelash. In most families, they know not to bring up certain subjects that arouse unpleasant memories. And no one gets seriously upset when children occasionally treat each other shabbily or parents complain about neglected household chores.

But when an old college classmate or a favorite aunt visits for the weekend, the situation becomes very different. The family brings out the guest towels and the good silver. Everyone puts on his or her best manners (that means burps are temporarily taboo), appears chastely attired, and showers the guest with attention, food and heart-warming entertainment. In other words, the house guest is to be treated royally and in a certain sense, the family is on trial. Indeed, it is the family's duty, if not privilege, to serve.

While entertaining the weekend guest, formalities are both bearable and functional. The host makes sure that polite euphemisms are used with guests and is careful not to cause discomfort or embarrassment. Unpleasant experiences are referred to cautiously and matters of health are inquired about ever so gently by stating rhetorically, "Please let us know if you need anything."

Neighborhood pals are another matter. When the children's friends come to visit—no matter what the purpose—it is the *visitors* who are on trial, who must prove themselves worthy of house privileges. Thus, knowing they must be on their best behavior, neighborhood friends tend to be polite, courteous and are rarely spoilsports.

Not only are neighborhood chums expected to learn and abide by the family rules, but they are also expected to know not to stay for dinner unless repeatedly invited, that certain areas of the house are off-limits and that teasing younger family members is *verboten*. Youngsters who overstep these invisible boundaries are labeled ill-mannered and when their behavior doesn't improve, they are admonished: Take your things and leave!

If the family has a cleaning lady, she is treated like neither a family member, honored guest nor neighborhood friend. Unlike the house guest and neighborhood chum who must limit their comings and goings to public areas, she is free to inspect every nook and cranny. It seems clear to everyone what the arrangement is: The housekeeper offers a cleaning service; the family offers payment—a basic trade-off.

When you think about it, the role of the housekeeper or cleaning lady is an intriguing paradox. She's both intimately involved with the family and at the same time extremely detached. In many ways she may know more about you and your family's business than your closest friend.

Yet families feign ignorance of the cleaning lady's presence or knowing eyes. What she sees and hears or thinks seems to matter naught, because everyone in the household assumes it's the cleaning lady's job to scrub, not scrutinize. Secondly, her status is such that family members would courteously disregard her opinions even if she were to offer any (live-in help and nannies are sometimes exceptions to this rule). And, perhaps most important, the cleaning lady has learned that her job is to see, but to pretend that she doesn't.

As you may gather, our ways of behaving at home vary greatly depending on whom we are with. We have distinct although familiar ways of relating to family, to house guests, to visiting neighbor friends and to hired help. *But what we don't have are familiar and traditional ways of relating to someone who comes from a foreign country for an extended stay in our home.*

Too often, host families try to place their new exchange student in one of the familiar roles that have just been described. Why? Because it's human nature to apply what we already know and are comfortable with to new situations. There is nothing wrong with this, of course, except for the fact that the exchange student-host family relationship does not fall into a familiar category. Trying to pretend that it does is like attempting to mold an extraordinary gem with an unusual shape into a traditional piece of jewelry. There is never a truly satisfying fit. And in the process, a marvelous opportunity to experience something entirely new is missed.

Let's look at why this is so.

FAMILY MEMBER ROLE

If exchange students could be brought home and somehow plugged in like a new toaster, then instantaneously and definitively they would become an integral part of a host family. But relationships and loyalties don't seem to happen that easily. Family bonds are created from participation in a common family culture of interwoven routines, years of shared experiences and a unique combination of intimacy, devotion, growth, conflict and loyalty.

When exchange students are encouraged prematurely to think of their hosts as family and are pressured to call their host parents Mom and Dad,[1] conflicts of allegiance can develop. The student may feel guilty for betraying his or her natural family by adopting a competing one or may worry that the hosts will feel rejected if they are not embraced in this honored way.

Of course, there are situations (especially after spending several months with a host family) when exchange students become so comfortable that they say they literally "feel like" a family member. But achieving this kind of closeness takes time, and at first, most students do not feel like a family member even if assured that they are. For example, when the family visits close relatives and reminisces with them, the student is likely to feel awkward. When holidays and birthdays are celebrated, the student may, at best, feel only partly involved. And, although students may eagerly attend church services to learn about U.S. religious practices, they are nonetheless apt to feel like outsiders.

HOUSE GUEST ROLE

For a host family to become excited about having a foreigner live in their home is pretty normal. Many families fret about whether they will do what's "right" to help the student feel comfortable during the first hours and days. And all families seem to work hard at extending an enthusiastic welcome. For all of these reasons—excitement, doubt, concern—host families frequently begin treating their exchange students as house guests. Wanting to please and entertain, they may unwittingly hoist the students up on a mighty throne. Cast as royalty, such students find it difficult to assume their roles as human beings who have the task of adjusting to a new living environment.

And what about the host family? The situation boils down to this: Realistically, how long can someone go without yawning or burping at the wrong time? Is it reasonable to assume that a host family can entertain, cater to, sacrifice for, play up to, and pamper an exchange student day after day for six weeks, six months or a full year? Our hunch is that by trying, nerves will soon get frazzled and resentments begin to fester.

Imagine what might happen if you begin treating the exchange student in your home like a house guest who is visiting for a three-day weekend. You obviously would not broach the subject of body functions to inquire whether or not the person is constipated from traveling. After all, you assume that a guest will know how to discreetly handle the situation.

You would courteously show house guests where the clean towels are kept, but you wouldn't need to demonstrate how to use the shower or toilet. The guest would have the following routine down pat: The shower curtain belongs on the inside of the tub, and the plumbing works well enough so that it's not necessary—as is customary in some parts of the world—to throw used toilet paper in the trash can. Moreover, while guests may wish to hand wash some items, most would not be staying so long that they would need to learn where to put dirty underwear or when to change the bed linens.

You also would not need to tell house guests where to buy tampons or how to dispose of them without clogging the drain pipes, or where to obtain birth control products.[2]

And what about finances? You can bet that a house guest will not arrive with eight hundred thousand cruzeiros (worth $2,000) stashed in a suitcase. You assume that the guest has traveler's checks and can handle money matters for the duration of the brief vacation. After all, a house guest can typically handle U.S. currency, and there would be no logical reason to suggest that a checking account be opened.

But with the arrival of an exchange student, many of these exquisitely sensitive, painfully intimate matters—matters which you rarely discuss with a house guest—may need addressing. On a few occasions in the past when these issues have been overlooked, families have found themselves dealing with dreadfully embarrassing problems.

NEIGHBORHOOD CHUM ROLE

Problems can also develop when an exchange student is viewed as a visiting neighborhood friend. Just as your family would be miserable trying to be gracious hosts for months on end, so is it nerve-racking for an exchange student who tries to be the forever obedient and polite visitor, alert day and night in order to avoid giving offense.

Also, if the family mistakenly believes that the student is here primarily to have a good time, how can the daily boring routines be camouflaged, or the serious moments jazzed up to make every second a roller coaster of thrills and excitement? Moreover, where can you send an exchange student who gets sick or sassy, since the student's home is not down the street or around the corner? Unlike the neighborhood youngster who visits for a few brief hours and then is gone, the exchange student stays on in your household.

CLEANING LADY ROLE

Few host families accept an exchange student with the obvious intent of acquiring live-in help—such as a babysitter, cleaning lady or handyman. Still, the expectations of some families are such that the student gets the impression that the relationship is purely one of exchanged services. This is the unspoken contract: The family agrees to provide room and board, and the student repays in gratitude by never complaining and doing whatever job is assigned. When reduced to traded services grounded in obligations, a relationship which initially brimmed with spontaneity and generosity can wither into something dry and bitter.

There's a second reason why exchange students don't make good cleaning ladies: They don't play by the rules for hired help. With an exchange student rummaging around and ultimately exploring every bottle and basket in a restless need to understand the new environment, the family has on its hands a cleaning lady or handyman with the curiosity of Sherlock Holmes! Students see, they acknowledge what they see and they put clues together to reach conclusions. Being on a par with the family, what the student sees and how she or he reacts may have a powerful effect. As one host parent expressed it, "At times, you feel yourself observed, painfully exposed and probably judged."

Some measure of uneasiness may be elicited by the prospect of being observed in the sanctity of your home, having your personal comfort jostled for more than a few days and talking about sensitive topics with the stranger who is your exchange student. If so, it is hardly surprising. It might reassure you to know that few experienced host families would describe the experience as a year of nothing but familiar warm feelings. Most say hosting is hard work, despite its yield of ample rewards.

Hosting an exchange student means relating to a visitor in a new way. The realization that there is no pre-packaged "set of rules" about how to proceed can be disconcerting. However, people who have been hosting for a number of years have thoughtfully observed and described some of the characteristics of host family-exchange student relationships. Their observations are offered in the following chapters, along with suggestions intended to provide guidance and encouragement for an enriching, enjoyable and successful hosting experience.

2. What Is Hosting All About?

The experience of host families suggests that the elements involved in hosting a foreign student can be summed up as follows:

- The student is here to learn about American family life from an insider's point of view but, although an inside learner, the student remains essentially an outsider to long-standing family ties, the family's shared history, and the special sense of loyalty felt exclusively by family members.

• As a learner and friend, the exchange student participates in the family's normal day-to-day activities. Through discussions, the student learns about the family's values, beliefs, outlook and historical roots. Over time and with continued involvement, the student usually develops a strong friendship with family members, a relationship of deep caring and high mutual regard.

• Through involvement with the family, the community and high school, the student builds a foundation for understanding the culture of the United States.

Thus, there appear to be two basic dimensions to hosting a foreign student: (1) sharing your lifestyle with a person from another country, and (2) providing a helping hand.

LIFESTYLE SHARING

Lifestyle sharing entails mapping out your particular style of living. Among other things, it means an awareness of and an ability to describe what you value in life and how those values are reflected in how you live—the things you do, the opinions you express and the company you keep. Of course, many things are learned by exchange students through the course of daily living. But the more these things are discussed and clarified, the better.

You might start identifying your lifestyle by asking yourself what lifts your spirits the most. Is it puttering in your vegetable garden, attending hockey games or jogging with your Sony Walkman? If none of the above fits for you, perhaps you enjoy pumping iron at the neighborhood health club, achieving computer literacy in a community college course, charging through a non-stop 60-hour work week or teaching a Sunday school class.

If you were polled, with what political persuasion, social causes, economic class, religious ideals or national symbols would you identify? What ethnic traditions and ancestry make up your family heritage? Is yours a family of doers or talkers or thinkers? How would you rate the importance of togetherness, achievement, open communication or affection?

In short, lifestyle sharing means revealing what you and your family are all about. From the vast array of themes in our culture, which one best describes you? And, since families vary within themes, what makes your particular family unique?

After having hosted half-a-dozen foreign students, this is how one couple describes the way they encourage an exchange student to participate in their family lifestyle:

> Before the first week is out, an exchange student living with us will begin to learn what makes us unique. We come from a strong Polish background and cherish some old-fashioned values. To look like slobs in the way we live, to sound like derelicts by using off-color language or to come across as goof-offs in the way we handle responsibilities would hurt our family pride tremendously.

They also point out the reasons why they are not a "Little America"—meaning that they are fairly typical of one kind of family but not representative of the whole country:

> We're a jump-in-and-do, on-the-go family. We're involved with our church, the youth group, with clubs and organizations, and we do what we can for our friends and neighbors. But we let our exchange student know right off that Americans are not all the same. We say, "Our culture is made up of a dozen or more major ingredients. Our family is just one of the vegetables—not the whole beef stew."

How does a family go about describing its lifestyle and cultural traditions? First of all, it can take hour upon hour of discussion and explanation—combined with regular reference to a good bilingual dictionary in search of words that aren't part of the exchange student's vocabulary. As the couple quoted above explains:

> It's quite time-consuming to host a foreign student. You just don't explain things in two or three words. Sometimes we're up 'til 3 in the morning trying to sort things out.

As this kind of sharing progresses between the family and the student, the necessary process of accommodation to each other begins. It is probably realistic to expect that the student will have to do most of the accommodating. After all, the student is moving into the host family's lifestyle and not vice versa. But some give and take by the host family is critically necessary. The host family we have already quoted continues:

> One year we had a French student who'd had her own apartment for two years. She'd grown accustomed to tossing dirty clothes in the closet, stacking dirty dishes in huge mounds and living in the same T-shirt and jeans for weeks on end. We tried our darndest to tolerate her ways, and we made some accommodations. But we had a clash of lifestyles until Nicole[1] felt she could comfortably conform to our particular style of housekeeping.

Another time we had a student who joined the local community theatre group. We were all excited for her but also stuck with a colossal scheduling dilemma. With my wife working evenings, our daughter taking dance lessons at 6 p.m. and our son going to Cub Scouts at 7, there was suddenly no way I could work out at the Y and get Brigetta to theatre practice. Things had to be reshuffled, and when I found myself driving to the playhouse four nights a week, I began to feel like a regular there. But we all understood that this was important for Brigetta. We have absolutely no regrets about it but think the statement, "Having an exchange student means just another mouth to feed," should be forever stricken from the books. It ain't necessarily so.

Lest this family leave the impression that talking about a lifestyle and making accommodations can be burdensome, rest assured that it is not. The family notes that satisfying returns come from the hard work, aggravation and long hours involved:

All in all, it can be a lot of fun showing another person what your life is like. On Easter, we take our exchange student with us to the parish where we have our basket of food blessed. On Christmas Eve, we'll all be in the kitchen throwing together strange kinds of foods like pierogi [stuffed Polish dumplings], and our exchange student will be with us, elbow to elbow, and throwing questions our way.

Our parents come from the old school and preach: "Don't get involved with strangers. If you need help or want friends, that's what family is for." But we have a different sense of family; our friendships are not just with relatives. We enjoy teenagers, and for us, it's important to share our home with people from around the world. That kind of connectedness with the world at large matters a whole lot to us.

Clearly, lifestyle sharing with a foreign student can be rewarding but is not necessarily as easy as making social conversation at a cocktail party or having an interesting chat with a tourist. When it comes to relating to adolescents in general and foreign students in particular, host families can find themselves readily challenged, occasionally burdened and frequently sought out for advice.

A HELPING HAND IN WONDERLAND

Many visitors to new countries and cultures experience a myriad of differences which can be confusing and sometimes seriously disorienting. In order to clarify how these differences affect people, let's take a look at an old story—Alice in Wonderland—from a new perspective.

When Alice tumbled down the rabbit hole and spiraled dizzily into Wonderland, she crashed with a muddled thump in a bizarre and mystifying realm where she bumped and stumbled her way among strange and eerie creatures. The humans Alice met seemed hardly humane. A grandiose duchess squeezed too close and muttered about "much of a muchness." "Take care of the sense, and the sounds will take care of themselves," Alice was chastised by people speaking a cacophony of platitudes, rhymes and riddles. "She's nervous. Execute her!" someone thundered when Alice shook and trembled with fear.

"You ought to be ashamed of asking such simple questions," a crowd shouted in her ear, leading Alice to blurt out in angry desperation, "There's no sense talking; these people are perfectly idiotic!" Lacking a book of rules to explain all the "frumious discomgollifustication" and feeling horribly confused, scolded and forsaken, Alice began stupidly bowing to anyone and everything, bobbing from the waist like an errant yo-yo.

As Alice described it, "Everything became curioser and curioser." "What's happening to me?" she asked herself, muffling her dread. "How strange everything is today, and yesterday things went on as usual. It was so much pleasanter at home where one wasn't always growing larger and smaller, and being ordered about by mice and rabbits. I almost wish I hadn't gone down that rabbit hole—and yet—and yet—it's rather curious, you know, this sort of life. When I used to read fairy tales, I fancied this kind of thing never happened, and now, here I am in the middle of one."

If Alice were to have a friendly chat with a panel of 20th Century social scientists, she might learn that when she left her familiar home and had feelings of alarm, confusion and homesickness in Wonderland, she had experienced a case of what is known among international sojourners as "culture shock."

Culture shock is a phrase which was popularized in 1958 by anthropologist Kalvero Oberg to describe the feelings of disorientation and anxiety that many people experience for a period of time while living in a foreign country. It results from the awareness that one's basic assumptions about life and one's familiar ways of behaving are no longer appropriate or functional.

When Alice entered Wonderland, she didn't know about culture shock, and she didn't think of Wonderland as a new and unfamiliar culture. But in a sense, that's what Wonderland was: a "foreign" culture where people related according to different expectations, where language was used differently to convey meaning and where the rules for polite and reasonable behavior were vastly different.

The social scientists might also suggest that it was indeed unfortunate that she had no one to turn to, no one to help bridge her home culture and that of Wonderland.

Like Alice, many exchange students go through culture shock— as if they too had stumbled into Wonderland. They might feel awkwardly oversized or shrunken with insecurity. The home where they stay can appear upside down and backwards. Keys from the culture they have left behind don't always unlock the doors to comfortable relationships and understanding. Confused and disoriented, just about everything may seem utterly mystifying and thoroughly bewildering for a while. Thus, exchange students often need help in the form of explanations, encouragement and guidance. In short, they need a "cultural advisor."

A cultural advisor is a person who is both familiar with the new culture and willing to help explain the behavior of its inhabitants. As a host parent who is an expert on your family's lifestyle and as someone knowledgeable about American culture, you probably will be the one your student turns to for assistance.

Sometimes it's a matter of correcting the way words are pronounced or how language is used. Imagine your exchange student arriving home from his first day at school. He rushes in the door and begins to recount the day's events by saying, "My chemistry class is on the turd floor."

You may cringe at the thought of having to explain the difference between "turd" and "third" even though you realize the embarrassment will only intensify if you ignore it.

During your foreign student's stay, you will probably be called upon repeatedly to define such things as the meaning of unfamiliar words, to interpret slang or to explain why describing one's sunny disposition by saying, "I'm a gay person," might be misinterpreted. When your exchange student continually asks about such things, you may begin to bristle and be tempted to cut him short.

Helping students with language is important when they will be misunderstood or embarrassed because of their errors. Otherwise, it is probably best, at least in the beginning, not to place too much emphasis on it. More important are the differences in behavior, attitudes and values which emerge over time as the student settles into life in this country. These emerging differences challenge the sojourner's basic assumptions about life and the belief that there is one right way for people to behave. When this happens, students can become confused, defensive and hypercritical, describing their host's lifestyle and culture as strange and illogical. But rather than discussing the basic issue of conflicting beliefs, students often complain instead about their hosts' quirks and inconsistencies:

- When you eat, why do you hold your fork so funny, with the prongs up instead of down?
- Why do you cover your mouth so politely when you yawn, but not when you hiccup?
- Why do you wash and rinse the dishes in separate containers yet bathe and rinse yourself in the same bath water?

Or they may mount a campaign of resistance against recognizing and accepting the differences—as was the case with one German student:

Axel was a charming, polite boy who made friends immediately. That was good, but I was worried. I fretted that he was going to visit a girl's home, invite himself into her bedroom and get thrown out by her father in two minutes flat.

So every day for two weeks, I told Axel that American teenagers do not entertain friends in their bedrooms like they do in Europe. For two weeks he didn't believe me; he argued, questioned and tried every possible way to explain away our custom.

His first reaction was to say, "If my English were better, I'm sure you'd agree with me. We're just not communicating." Next he discredited me and said, "You're crazy! You've got to be the only American who thinks like that." And he began bargaining with statements like, "Surely you're not talking about the daytime too, or with the door open." Then he just plain rejected what I said, "Well, that's stupid! The European way is better."

For all that time, what I was telling Axel just bounced off. Finally, after he had passed through all these mental steps, he accepted what I said as an accurate and sane message: "In the U.S., no boys in girls' bedrooms, no girls in boys' bedrooms. That's the rule."

Sometimes exchange students find the differences so immense or improbable that they wonder if they are free-floating through time and space. Flávio, a thoughtful young Brazilian, felt so swept away by incomprehensible differences that he exclaimed:

In the U.S., water swirls down the drain clockwise instead of the counterclockwise Brazilian way, your coffee tastes like dish water, the Southern Cross is missing from the night sky, the girls swear and talk about sex and students are friends with their teachers. When I saw all this, I became lost in space. I thought: "How can this be? I am really in a very different place!"

What lies behind these new cultural experiences and why is the role of a cultural advisor so important? The principal source of the problem is that students bring with them a load of "cultural baggage" by which they instinctively attempt to live while in their new cultural environment.

3. Cultural Baggage: What the Customs Inspector Doesn't See

Perhaps you've already had the experience of being at the airport for the arrival of a colorful entourage of weary but wide-eyed exchange students. Although dressed in the usual teenage garb of designer jeans and baggy T-shirts, their foreignness is rarely disguised; it is telegraphed by their uncommon gestures, their darting glances, the musical lilt to their voices and their quizzical "Where am I?" stares.

As the students go through customs, the inspectors open suitcases, rummage through clothing, examine an occasional guitar case and peer into packages and dog-eared cardboard boxes. Everything visible to the scrutinizing eye is checked. But there is something more that exchange students bring with them, something not so immediately obvious as highly visible suitcases, souvenirs and flight bags. They also bring the beliefs, the attitudes and the rules for proper behavior that they have learned at home. Each student's combination of these personal and cultural characteristics constitutes what we are calling "cultural baggage."

It is only after exchange students have crossed the threshold, unpacked and stored their suitcases that this invisible baggage gradually begins to appear. Some of the ways invisible baggage becomes obvious are described on the following pages.

In the middle of the night, a Mexican girl named Margarita became worried that her American host father was planning to seduce her. It turned out the father had given the girl a goodnight kiss and hug—something he routinely did with his own children. He innocently assumed his behavior would convey to Margarita nothing more than fatherly affection. But Margarita didn't think of him as her father and wasn't used to expressions of affection from males outside of her natural family. She considered his behavior inappropriate and threatening.

Another standard that differs from culture to culture is the attitude about what is considered proper attire, especially the way one dresses in casual situations around the house.

An American student staying with a Colombian family was viewed by his hosts as indiscreet. "Robert didn't bring a bathrobe, pajamas or slippers," contended the señora. "He'd sleep in shorts and just put on his trousers to go to the bathroom. I didn't like this."[1] Similarly, a student from Australia by the name of Rachel was accustomed to dashing about her natural family's home in a sheer nightgown; her parents thought nothing about it. In fact, attitudes about nudity generally are more liberal in Australia, and nude bathing on some beaches is the norm. But Rachel's American family felt quite differently: They concluded that she was being flirtatious and seductive with her host father and brothers.

A Chilean exchange student found that his cultural baggage spilled out at the dinner table. "Ricardo was selfish," his American host mother concluded. "He would take two pork chops, and then the platter would be empty when it reached the last person around the table."

Ricardo hadn't recognized one of his host family's cultural assumptions: One pork chop is the appropriate amount of meat, and when the platter contains one chop per person, taking more is considered greedy. Instead, he was still functioning as though he were with his natural family in Chile where "appropriate" was defined as the amount of food necessary to satisfy the appetite—whether that meant one or two or three pork chops per person. Knowing that, Ricardo's natural mother and the family maid always prepared enough pork chops to meet individual needs.

Ricardo's host family, on the other hand, based their definition of appropriate on the notion that meat is a semi-luxury to be eaten sparingly. The host family planned their meals around this definition, but they never thought to explain it to their exchange student.

Food is particularly important in the hosting relationship since it often carries a heavy burden of cultural meaning. Sometimes it is used to express hospitality. It also can express such things as "love" (giving chocolates on Valentine's Day), "celebration" (toasts with sparkling champagne), "poverty" (beans and rice are considered peasant food by some Brazilians) and "thank-you" (a gift of bottled herring!).

One American host family learned the hard way that certain foods also express contempt. When they served their German student corn on the cob, he stood up and left the table. Only after a long discussion was it clarified that for most Germans, it has traditionally been an insult to serve corn at the dinnertable; in Germany, corn was until recently considered to be barnyard food.

A different kind of misunderstanding developed between an American host family and a student named Eduardo. He had concluded that his family was cold and boring, and the family had concluded that they had been sent a rowdy student who was making selfish demands that he be constantly entertained. "Eduardo wants the U.S. to be just a big party," his host father complained. Eduardo retorted by exclaiming, "This place is as dead as a cemetery."

What Eduardo and his family did not understand was that they each had a different culturally-based pattern of socializing. Because he was familiar with the hustle and bustle of a Latin American city, Eduardo was accustomed to meeting frequently with friends and extended family for get-togethers which often lasted late into the night.[2] By contrast, his American host family's concept of socializing involved quiet evenings together watching favorite T.V. shows and talking with friends after church on Sunday.

Invisible baggage can also include the way one goes about disagreeing with another person. In many American families, it may be the rule that outright arguing with parents is unacceptable, but children are allowed to complain and "talk their way out of" doing certain things they don't like. But in an exchange student's culture and family, it might not be appropriate to ever complain verbally.

If a Brazilian is unwilling to go along with a parent's request, instead of questioning, "Why do I have to?" he'll be more inclined to respond, "Maybe," or "O.K., I'll do it later," and assume it's understood he plans to do it NEVER! Similarly, a Malaysian girl might disagree by saying "yes" verbally but saying "no" in her grimacing facial expression.

It's not that Brazilian and Malaysian teenagers never disagree with adults. It's that each culture has different definitions of what the "respectful" way to disagree is. Consequently, if cultural cues are misread, each side can wrongly conclude that they are dealing with someone dishonest, irrational or rude.

What each of the above examples portrays is the complex nature of cross-cultural interaction. Typically, each party is unaware that the other person has a different way of looking at the situation— just as happened with Alice and the inhabitants of Wonderland when they tried to relate to each other. What's more, the misunderstandings that occur can involve seemingly minor details that one would think could easily be ignored or excused. But the significance of these minor details is often amplified, as is noted by Ray Gorden, a researcher who studied communication patterns during the homestays of Americans in Colombia:

> Often we tend to simplistically assume that misunderstandings over "trivial matters" would not lead to any serious consequences between people of intelligence and goodwill. Yet, we have considerable evidence that both the Americans and Colombians drew rather basic conclusions about the others' character as a result of "trivial" misinterpretations. Few Americans realized that such "trivia" led the majority of Colombian hosts to conclude that their [students] were "generally thoughtless of others," that "they think they are superior," and that "they do not care about their reputation among Colombians."[3]

Quite understandably, you'll never actually "see" an exchange student's—or anyone else's—cultural baggage. We become aware of it only indirectly in the everyday behavior it produces. The dilemma for students is that behavior which was so logical, proper and correct back home doesn't "work" in the U.S., which has its own equally logical, proper and correct set of behaviors.

4. What You Need To Know About Culture

In the process of serving as a cultural advisor and helping students with their cultural baggage, something more grows out of the experience. As one mother put it:

> Whenever you work together to reach a new understanding about some cultural difference, a mispronounced word, some confusing behavior or a shocking new experience, you'll feel a sense of accomplishment. This is not accomplishment for having solved a particular problem, but accomplishment in terms of helping the relationship go one step deeper.
>
> When I notice us moving in closer on the couch, when we can laugh about crazy situations, when we become comfortable with silent moments—all these things tell me the relationship is going well, and it really feels right. All at once I think, "Oh, boy! This exchange student is really somebody who belongs in my life."

To fulfill your role as a cultural advisor as you move toward a deeper relationship, it will be helpful for you to know something about how culture influences our lives.

By culture, we refer to what is sometimes called "deep culture"[1]—the largely intangible and implicit patterns of behavior that govern the lives of different societies and groups of people. It includes the group's world views, ways of expressing emotions, predominant attitudes and sanctioned forms of behavior. In this definition, we are not referring to what may be more popular definitions of culture: "high culture" (the performing and visual arts, formal etiquette and a liberal arts education) or "folk culture" (oral traditions, cuisine, folk dances, songs, parables and proverbs).

The patterns of "deep culture" are assimilated by every member of the group and, through enculturation (imitation and unconscious learning processes), exert a strong influence over the way people live. Although all people have certain common needs and desires, no two cultures respond to human needs in exactly the same way; each develops its own unique patterns.

To further explain the impact of culture, described below are five major areas which are strongly influenced by a person's enculturation: perceptions, assumptions, communication patterns, ethnocentrism and stereotyping.

PERCEPTIONS

People in a given culture tend to view events in the same way without ever realizing that they hold common perceptions that differ from culture to culture. For example, when they watch T.V. sitcoms, most Americans are attuned to the plot and jokes. But a foreigner watching the same American T.V. program for the first time may be attuned to the dubbed-in laugh tracks—a facet of the show Americans usually don't notice at all. Why does the foreigner notice what most Americans don't? Because people see and hear in a selective fashion without realizing that they have been culturally conditioned to notice only certain aspects of any given situation.

ASSUMPTIONS

It is important to realize that people in different cultures tend to have their own common assumptions about what's meaningful and important in life. When Brazilians remark that Americans are "work crazed and cold," the comment is the result of norms and assumptions that are specific to Brazilian culture. As a general rule, Brazilians approach their work and their relationships in what they believe are more "practical" ways. But Americans have their own culture-based definitions of what is "practical," and as a result, they sometimes see Brazilians as "undisciplined and hedonistic."

COMMUNICATION PATTERNS

It's fairly obvious that people in different countries may speak different languages, but it is not so obvious that people from other cultures may have different thought processes: some use an entirely different system of logic, while others recognize certain experiences for which our language provides no equivalent. For example, the Japanese have two dozen or more forms for the English pronoun "I." The one used depends on who is talking, to whom, and what the social relationship between them is. Our language does not allow us the option of communicating respect or deference in this manner. Thus, the way languages are constructed can create realities that differ vastly from one culture to another.

There are also significant cultural differences in how people use eye contact, a smile, a hand gesture or physical space to convey meaning. For example, a person from Singapore may express deference and respect by averting his eyes, lowering his voice and allowing periods of silence. But Americans are "taught" by their culture that this behavior communicates disrespect and deviousness. We are admonished to "speak up and look people in the eye."

ETHNOCENTRISM

Once people have acquired the perceptions, assumptions and communication patterns of their own particular culture, they tend to become ethnocentric—unaware that there are equally valid alternatives and convinced that their cultural patterns are the only "natural" and "reasonable" way for human beings to live.

As a result, each different culture has a tendency to view outsiders as inferior people who arrogantly boast about being superior. These ethnocentric attitudes contribute to the formation of stereotypes—descriptions that may hold some truth but tend to be overgeneralized and are often either demeaning or ultra-positive.

STEREOTYPING

When people are asked about other countries, they often use descriptions that are indicative of positive or negative stereotypes. A Newsweek Magazine[2] poll conducted by the Gallup Organization in six nations—Brazil, Great Britain, France, Japan, Mexico and West Germany—investigated attitudes toward Americans as a people, the influence of American lifestyles and U.S. foreign policy. In each country, those polled generally approved of Americans; they agreed that American influence on the world is growing, and many said they embraced American products and the popular American culture of blue jeans, McDonald's and T.V. shows like "Dallas."

But each of these cultures drew on different stereotypes to describe us. According to the poll, the French see us as a decisive, industrious and inventive people, but they give us low marks in honesty and sophistication. To the Japanese, we are seen as nationalistic, friendly, decisive, rude and self-indulgent. The West Germans describe us as energetic, inventive, friendly, sophisticated and intelligent, but not very sexy. The British, however, view us as a people who are energetic and friendly but also nationalistic, self-indulgent and not very sophisticated. Like the British, the Brazilians view us as energetic, but they also describe us as greedy and not very sexy or sophisticated. The Mexicans describe us as intelligent, industrious, inventive and greedy. But like the French, they don't rate us high on honesty.

It might be helpful to know that there are a number of stereotypes which many exchange students recite when describing Americans. In general, we are seen as: hard working, ignorant of other cultures, generous, always in a hurry, boastful, highly materialistic, innovative and suffering from a superiority complex.

At some point, discussions of these stereotypes can help exchange students reach a more accurate view of Americans. These talks also help students realize that they can understand Americans without necessarily liking all that Americans represent. From the host family's perspective, the discussions can serve to challenge the belief that Americans are perfect and should be loved by everyone.

5. The Adolescent Sojourner's Experience

Just as all of us have our ups and downs in life, so do exchange students. But for them, the ups may be a little higher and the downs a little lower. After all, not only are exchange students adolescents going through major growing pains, but they are also international sojourners who have temporarily left behind their homes, families, friends and countries.

Let us again emphasize that we are not suggesting that there is a set of experiences through which all students go. Since no two persons are alike, we can't say exactly how any individual exchange student will adjust to life in the U.S. Each student adjusts at a different pace, each family responds differently, and together they create their own special patterns of reactions and relationships. Nevertheless, there are many experiences which *are* common among exchange students and certain stages through which many if not most of them go. Highlighting these can help families deal more effectively with the challenges of hosting even though their own experiences may be somewhat different.

Most students begin their visit to the U.S. on a high note and go through a number of ups and downs before their departure.[1] The reasons for these highs and lows are explained in this chapter. Then, in Chapters 7 through 15, we offer some suggestions for helping an exchange student who is going through the peaks and valleys of cultural adjustment.

ARRIVAL FATIGUE

Newly arrived exchange students are often at the peak of an emotional high. Months of preparation have culminated in a jet flight across international borders. They have also experienced the burst of excitement that comes from meeting their new host families for the first time. The host family usually is just as excited and often has already made plans to assure that the student meets almost everyone and sees almost everything as soon as possible. Thus, the host family sets in motion a flurry of fun-packed festivities and scenic tours.

In many cases, however, it isn't long before the student begins looking glassy-eyed, yawning drowsily and responding only halfheartedly, causing the family to feel confused and mildly insulted. "Sure, he's a little tired from traveling," the family acknowledges. "But if he really wanted to, he could overcome it and enjoy being here."

What families might not realize is that during these first days, their student has arrived physically, but that's about all. On the inside, many students feel "lost in space" and mildly miserable with the symptoms of what we have called arrival fatigue. Jet lag and the discomforts of long international flights have caught up with them. Although they have been welcomed into an American home, they pace and fidget with the awkwardness of being a stranger in an unfamiliar place. Cut off from their families and familiar surroundings, many of the students feel lost in a collection of new free-floating experiences.

In addition, students often succumb to a kind of language overload that comes from straining to understand and speak English. As one student put it, "I thought I would scream if I heard one more word of English. It felt like bombs were going off in my head!" Communicating becomes a little like trying to converse under water; people may be talking, but what comes through is a mere babble of gargles and gurgles. "I would try to understand," a student notes, "but the words just flew past my head."

How long does arrival fatigue last? Some students begin to recover after just a few days and have only mild symptoms for the next while. Others, especially those who begin school immediately, might experience arrival fatigue for a month or longer. Eventually, when they have recovered and learned enough to move about with some ease, an optimism surfaces.

SETTLING IN

Rather than focusing on the differences between life at home and life in the new culture, it seems that sojourners initially pay more attention to the similarities. Consequently, an exchange student soon recognizes that in certain ways, Americans are just like everyone else: they eat meals, work, shop, study, watch T.V. and drive cars. Recognizing these similarities serves to help students feel comfortable with the U.S. "Everything is just fine," a student might say at this point. Of course, some cultural differences might be noted but with a bemused reaction such as, "How quaint," or "How interesting."

In time, however, the differences between cultures become increasingly noticeable, and the potential for culture shock emerges. In addition, exchange students sometimes have unrealistic expectations for their sojourn, and letting go of these expectations can be unsettling.

Overly positive expectations come in many guises, sometimes sending students in search of such things as "perfect" host parents or a family experience that is tension-free and brimming with boundless affection. As lovely as they may seem, these unrealistic expectations can cause an otherwise promising experience to go awry.

A more common, though equally unrealistic, expectation is that their foreignness will automatically transform them into special people. They sometimes expect to be showered with attention in the classroom, enthusiastically embraced by the popular kids and invited to join the high status cliques. When they are at times received with disinterest or even ridicule, they can become crestfallen and disillusioned.

Another faulty expectation is that the student and the family will share a Hollywood lifestyle. Since many exchange students know about the U.S. only from what they have seen in movies, they at times erroneously expect their host families to live like flashy movie stars who own lavish mansions, dash off to Las Vegas nightclubs on weekends and entertain the jet set at posh parties. Similarly, they might expect the children in these families to be freewheeling and zany. Explained one Colombian exchange student: "I was nervous about coming to the U.S. From the movies, I thought American teenage girls went to orgies and led a wild life."

Many foreign exchange students are from large cosmopolitan centers and sometimes encounter surprises of a different kind. They expect to find U.S. towns and communities that are bustling with activity, equipped with modern rapid transit systems, and futuristic in outlook and design. They are not prepared for the fact that many host families enjoy a slower-paced, small-town atmosphere or the simplicity of a tranquil farm community.

DEEPENING THE RELATIONSHIP

As we have seen, students are inevitably going to be uncertain about what to do, how to behave and how to deal with relationships within the family. The rules and codes by which they managed relationships in their own homes are going to be inadequate as guidelines. This is a period, then, in which they will be fumbling, testing, exploring and experimenting. But in the process, deeper relationships develop as the family clarifies its lifestyle and defines its "rules" for daily living.

CULTURE SHOCK

The stage is set for culture shock when the thrill of the arrival fades, dreams become frayed at the edges and the new culture no longer seems just like home with a few differences. A student might begin to reason:

> Sure, Americans eat meals like the folks back home, but why is American food so bland, and why does my host family eat so much of it so fast?
>
> Yes, Americans work, but why do they work such long hours, and why can't my host father at least relax on weekends like my father at home?
>
> Sure, Americans shake hands, but it seems to be routine with men and uncertain with women. How am I supposed to know when it's O.K. to shake hands and when it's not?"

There are at least two probable reasons why culture shock occurs. One is the realization that much of what happens in the new environment strikes the sojourner as erratic and senseless. Quite often, one's customary way of thinking can produce confusion rather than understanding, and one's normal behavior might look unacceptably strange and abnormal.

The other cause is somewhat ironic; culture shock's greatest impact may come not as a reaction to the new culture, but from the sojourner's heightened awareness of the idiosyncracies in one's own culture and the ways one is culture bound.[2] No matter what the cause, however, the result is generally the same: The traveler begins to feel helpless and anxious. When this happens, the sojourner may find it difficult to function well and may experience some unpleasant psychological reactions. This decline has been described in the cross-cultural literature as the first part of a U-shaped curve of adjustment[3] as portrayed by the dotted line in the figure below.

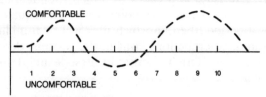

DURATION OF HOMESTAY BY MONTHS

The helplessness and anxiety of culture shock can manifest itself in unusual actions, emotional extremes or frightening thoughts. Some people become excessively concerned about cleanliness and begin to bathe or shower repeatedly. Others might become overly preoccupied about sickness or safety. Smoking often increases as does eating, although some people lose their appetite almost completely. Insomnia and oversleeping are fairly common behavior changes. Emotional reactions can include withdrawal, irritability, moodiness or exaggerated elation.

Researchers aren't sure why, but some people never experience culture shock at all, others recover in a matter of weeks or months, some take up to a year or longer to recover and a few find it virtually impossible to overcome and choose instead to return home. In addition, some people experience culture shock but prefer not to discuss it, possibly because admitting that they are feeling helpless and confused might be misinterpreted as a sign of personal weakness or immaturity.

The wide variety of reactions to culture shock makes it important to emphasize that while we want to describe the typical experiences of sojourners, we can't say exactly what will happen to any particular student. If our concept of the culture shock experience fits your student, then the patterns we are describing should be helpful to you. If it doesn't fit, then you can use it as a measure by which to assess your own experience. Here are five of its major dimensions:

Identity Crisis. Like Alice in Wonderland, travelers to foreign countries can have a hard time figuring out what is going on. It might seem to an exchange student that Americans laugh at the wrong time, get excited about trivial matters, ask embarrassing questions, or don't know how to express friendship even if they're always smiling. That's because the two cultures may differ in defining when it's appropriate to laugh, what events are meaningful and should arouse an enthusiastic response, what topics are too private to discuss or how to convey respect and make friends.

When students don't know what to do or when to do it, their sense of self-confidence and identity can be shaken; in fact, students sometimes feel so confused that they wonder who they really are. "My host family doesn't know who I am," one student declared, "and neither do I."

Atypical Behavior. When culture shock begins, host families sometimes wonder if someone switched students on them. That person who was so friendly and outgoing can turn sullen or cling like a frightened child. It can be quite disturbing to try reasoning with someone who over-reacts, under-reacts, makes harsh judgments, isn't logical or has scaled the pinnacle of stubbornness by insisting absolutely, "I'm NOT going through culture shock!"

Anger. When confused, sojourners often find it comforting to put the blame on someone or something else, and one of the easiest targets available to a foreign sojourner is the new culture. After all, things were fine until arrival on foreign soil, so blame oozes out in the form of complaints and irritability. "This culture (or country, or place) is bad," reasons the student, "because it makes me feel bad." The counterpart to a student's intolerance for the new culture is exaggerated praise for one's home culture. "My country's way of doing things," the sojourner might boast, "is so much better." In a few cases of culture shock, sojourners angrily reject most aspects of the culture they have left behind and "go native." "Everything in the U.S. is so wonderful," they might exude, "and everything at home is so awful."

Mourning. The very nature of being an exchange student means that the things one dearly loves—parents, home, friends—have been left thousands of miles behind. Quite understandably, many students react with feelings of sadness. That's why certain students retreat to their bedrooms or become noticeably moody.

However they go about it, most students need some time to experience feelings of loss. Psychiatrist A. Cesar Garza-Guerrero says this is a normal process which makes it possible for sojourners to free themselves emotionally from their home culture and temporarily find comfort in a new place.[4]

Recovery. With the resolution of the feelings that are characteristic of culture shock, the sojourner becomes less judgmental and more accepting of the differences between the home and host cultures. When this shift occurs, cultural differences are seen not as good or bad; they are viewed as opportunities to learn something new.

Recovery, however, is rarely sudden. It is generally a slow process, punctuated by improvement and minor declines; just when everything seems back to normal, the sojourner might come up against some new problem which causes the confused feelings to return for a momentary flourish. But increasingly, as the student gets more involved with the family, the new culture no longer seems so foreign and forbidding. (For detailed information about culture shock, see Chapter 11.)

THE HOLIDAYS

Students on year-long exchange programs almost always arrive in the U.S. just before school begins in the late summer. Three or four months later—about when most of them are emerging from culture shock—the holiday season arrives.

For many students, the holidays bring a longing for family and friends and an awareness of being an outsider in the midst of merriment and celebration. These uncomfortable feelings can trigger a return of culture shock symptoms: homesickness, irritability, fearfulness and withdrawal. In some cases, the unpleasant reactions that surface during the holidays can linger into January or occasionally longer.

For other students, the holiday season stirs only a barely noticed tinge of culture shock. And some sail unperturbed right through Christmas and New Year's, possibly because their important holidays fall somewhere else on the calendar, or because they already feel quite settled in the new culture.

CULTURE LEARNING

Students start learning about the host's lifestyle and about American culture the moment they arrive. But an indepth exploration of cultural differences often gets delayed until culture shock passes and a period of culture learning begins.

Many host families report that going through the culture learning stage with an exchange student is one of the most enjoyable aspects of hosting. The long talks that were necessary to explain family rules and routines now give way to easy conversations and good times spent together. A deep interpersonal relationship often develops between the family and the student, resulting in rich emotional and intellectual experiences as each makes new discoveries about the other.

PRE-DEPARTURE

As the end of the homestay experience approaches, a mixture of feelings may emerge: enthusiasm about farewell parties and graduation activities, apprehension about saying goodbye, excitement about returning to loved ones back home, concern about having changed so much that acceptance at home will be difficult, and doubts about whether others will understand how one person could be in such a state of confusion. Here's how one student expressed his ambivalence:

> I'm going back. I can hardly wait. But what's my Mom going to look like? Will my sisters be taller? What if I speak with an American accent? Will my friends accept the new me? Will my American host family still love me after I've left and am far, far away?

READJUSTMENT

Upon returning home, sojourners typically surge to another emotional high—a euphoric peak that comes from being reunited with family and friends. Yet, inevitably, the student notices that much has changed—perhaps the returnee most of all. So once again, the "Who am I?" questions emerge, leading to another emotional slump which is known as reverse culture shock or re-entry shock.

As with culture shock, reverse culture shock is an experience of disorientation and anxiety. Only this time, it's the student's home culture and natural family which are the sources of discomfort. There can even be a mourning process as a student longs for a family—in this case, the host family—and for a culture which have been left behind.

Experts in the field say many students find reverse culture shock to be the bumpiest part of the entire exchange experience. But eventually, most students can look back on the totality of their experience and agree with a student who said:

> In the United States I crossed hard times and difficult understanding. My culture shock was more than a word. But I had a wonderful American family. They loved me like their son, and I loved them back.
>
> I didn't think all this could happen in such a short time. I never laughed or cried or learned so much. In the United States I became a man with myself; I went there to get my adult, and I got it.

6. The Host Family's Experience

Americans do not travel to a distant land when they host an exchange student. But many families experience intense and sometimes upsetting reactions as a result of having in their home a person who represents a totally different way of life. The behavior of exchange students can seem incomprehensible at times, their ideas can be shocking, and their questions can challenge fundamental beliefs about what are the "right" ways to live or think. When this happens, the family can go through a kind of culture shock reaction of its own.

Because we know of no single word that conceptualizes the family's reactions, we have coined the term "exchange-itis" to represent this quasi-culture shock experience:

> EXCHANGE-ITIS is a mild to severe condition experienced by families who take in foreign exchange students, an inflammation of the host family's routines, composure, outlook and convictions. It is the family's parallel condition to the exchange student's culture shock. Symptoms: irritability, elation or discouragement, and at times, a loss of objectivity
>
> ONSET: Families know they are getting exchange-itis when their student begins to seem like a jack-in-the-box who startles them with a surprising

question, unusual behavior, unconventional opinion or beautiful experience.

ANTIDOTE: 1) Relaxing with the idea that going through quasi-culture shock is a normal part of being a host parent; 2) Entering the experience informed and prepared.

Granted, we are being a bit playful, but many former host families have suggested that a new host family sort of "catches" a mysterious affliction which influences or "contaminates" their outlook and beliefs.

One host mother's initial tinge of quasi-culture shock brought on an emotional high. Being an opera singer who loves Japanese art, the mother became enthralled by her Japanese exchange student's exquisitely delicate, porcelain-like face: "I would see Michi enter the room and have a wonderful feeling of being connected with centuries of living oriental art."

Families who host Middle Eastern students may have a mild exchange-itis experience before the morning coffee has been perked. One host mother who got up early to prepare a scrumptious breakfast for the family and their newly-arrived student recalled the following embarrassing eye opener:

> I'd just started cooking when Abdul walked in, got a whiff of the bacon and blanched. In a curiously repelled voice he asked, "What's that smell?"
> After five minutes of ghastly silence, it dawned on me: Muslims don't eat pork. I thought, "Oh my gosh! I know that. Why didn't I think of it?"

In another situation, a host father swung by the house one weekday afternoon to pick up some business papers. As he dashed by the kitchen window, something on the lawn caught his eye. It was his Swedish exchange student, Inge, sunbathing entirely in the buff. "Now THAT took some adjustment!" exclaimed the host father, his eyes widening with laughter:

> When I walked into that situation, I ended up doing more than shouting, "Hey, get some clothes on, Inge." I was hit really hard by the clash of cultural standards. I began to consider the whole notion of what's decent and why.

Surprises like these can cause host parents to question aspects of their own particular lifestyle, compare cultural traits and eventually begin to understand things from a totally new perspective. But in the process of learning, families can begin to feel exposed and sometimes find their beliefs somewhat shaken. The following is an explanation of how this happens.

A HOUSE OF MIRRORS

To stay afloat in the stormy waters of life's compromises and complex realities, adults often drop anchor in protected harbors. They adopt a policy of ignoring, tolerating and excusing. Teenagers come along with their youthful zest and exaggerated idealism to rock the boat of parental complacency and occasional cop-outs. They sometimes interrogate their parents with piercing and intimidating questions about topics adults would prefer quietly to ignore.

When parents try to reform their kids but engage in certain vices themselves, their teenage children may ask: "How come you keep lecturing me about how bad marijuana is? You always have a drink when you're uptight." Or, occasional grumbling about hating a job might be confronted with: "Why do you continue working there? Why don't you have the guts to quit?"

Teenagers can be deadeyes for adult hypocrisies and foibles. They stand opposite to us, raising to our faces a life-sized mirror which reflects back our frailties and forces us to look and see ourselves as we really are.

How might the "adolescent-as-mirror" phenomenon affect the hosting experience? Many host families report that inviting a teenage exchange student into the home can multiply the mirror phenomenon tenfold. Almost nothing that is said or done will escape scrutiny by the exchange student. Not only can you as a host parent be gently nudged into acknowledging your personal flaws and inconsistencies, but you might also find yourself floundering when your views are solicited about politics, thorny social issues or American cultural values.

You may not find an easy answer or quick escape when asked questions such as the following:

- Why do you watch so much T.V. and stuff yourself with junk food from fastfood joints?
- What are you doing to eliminate poverty and racism in the U.S.?
- Why are you so hung-up about free love?
- If the baseball play-offs are between two American teams, why do you call it the World Series?

– Since the U.S. has only 12% of the world's population, what gives it the right to consume nearly two-thirds of the earth's natural resources?

Some old-timers at hosting foreign students say that these kinds of questions can seize you by the scruff of the neck and give you and your values a thorough shaking up. To endure and grow from such questions, it helps if:

– Over the years, you've cast your beliefs not in stone but rather in something a little more flexible.

– You can tolerate critical comments without arguing back, apologizing, or trying to convert others to your way of life.

– You welcome the opportunity to examine what you stand for and why.

– You delight in exchanges with adolescents because you enjoy their intensity, their candor, their rambunctiousness and their questions, which can effectively turn your home into a "house of mirrors."

LOSS OF CULTURAL INNOCENCE

Most of us can recall when we first learned there was no Santa Claus or heard our first dirty joke or discovered where babies come from. Each time we had one of those experiences (and there were thousands of them), we were losing a bit of our childhood innocence. That innocence initially served a critical purpose: it protected us from biological and psychological realities which—if presented too early in life—could have been overwhelming and destructive. As we matured physically and emotionally, we gradually shed our innocence and in exchange gained the knowledge and understanding that made us self-reliant and responsible adults.

While growing into and through adulthood, we also typically lose our innocence about social and political issues. We are disturbed to learn that some doctors are get-rich quacks, some clergymen abscond with church funds or their neighbor's wife, some GI's torched peasant huts in Vietnam, and presidents sometimes scorch the oval office of the White House with coarse and insulting language. We can blind ourselves to these realities or we can acknowledge them—ugly as they may be—and in the end grow wiser and more tolerant, or at least more prudent about whom we choose as our doctors, ministers, military commanders and political leaders.

Not always, but very often, bringing a foreign student into the home can stretch one's loss of innocence another giant step, exposing family members to international realities that go far beyond the immediate family, community, culture and nation.

As a host parent, you might not want your children to know about free love, only to host a European girl who has openly lived with an older man. You might never have given much thought to the havoc wreaked by World War II, only to receive a German boy who wants to discuss and argue the nuances of Nazism and its defeat by the Allies. Yours might be a deeply religious family, only to have a youngster who belongs to a religion you know nothing about, who has no religion at all or who is strongly opposed to religion.

You might abhor the idea of sodomy, yet have your family learn from your exchange student that it's quite acceptable and widely practiced in some cultures. You might want your children to promote equality and justice for all but have a student whose family has built up fortunes beyond belief by supporting exploitative and oppressive dictatorships. Or, you might have heard people say the U.S. has the world's highest standard of living, only to encounter a Scandinavian student whose country far exceeds the U.S. in certain areas of health care, social services and per capita income.

Of course, you might not have any of these experiences, but each is a real-life example. And almost every exchange student will say or do something at some point which has the effect of ungluing one's cultural certainties. An American host mother describes what happened to her:

> Being persecuted for one's Jewishness was just something I'd read about in a history book. For me, it didn't happen to real people. Then we had Jorge, an exchange student from Argentina. His grandparents had narrowly escaped being gassed in a Nazi concentration camp, and their story had been told and retold by the family.
>
> Jorge relived these horrors in frequent nightmares. My husband and I were shocked to see his pain. So we suffered too.
>
> When we gave him a Star of David pendant for graduation, we thought he'd feel proud. But Jorge wasn't. "My parents have forbidden me to wear this. It's not wise for Jews to be marked, to be singled out in this way," he advised us.
>
> Seeing the living history that tormented Jorge forced me to participate in a deeper knowledge. No longer could I be a mere bystander to history.

We would suggest that you seriously consider what it might be like for your family to lose its cultural innocence. It might mean discovering that some of your treasured and long-held beliefs about the U.S. and other countries are only as solid as a sandcastle lapped by ocean waves.

Hopefully, any loss of cultural innocence will create in you positive changes similar to those described by one host mother:

> Before we hosted a student, we were in the dark ages about our family, life in the U.S., other cultures and America's impact on the world. We may not do any better on geography tests, but our view of the world has definitely changed. I don't think we could ever be persuaded that one way of life is categorically right. We've lost our belief in uncontestable, absolute, singular opinions. We've moved into a world with a hundred shades of grey in it, and for us, there's absolutely no backing up from that.

HOW LONG DOES THE FAMILY'S QUASI-CULTURE SHOCK LAST?

Experienced families say there's a good chance that the family's version of culture shock will start out mildly and then intensify two or three months into the homestay before it begins to ease up. By the mid-way point, few symptoms may remain. But to some extent, it probably will be around as long as there is an exchange student in the home.

"At first everything was perfect. But after we'd had Juan awhile, the honeymoon feelings vanished," states one host mother who began to notice things that were either surprising or upsetting. A host father occasionally found himself "fed-up" and began asking: "Why did we make this decision? What am I getting out of this experience except aggravation?" Explains a third host parent:

> When things suddenly aren't wonderful any longer, that's usually a sign that the family has entered a period of intense learning and adjustment. It helps an awful lot if the family understands what's happening and can see the benefits of it.

How much or how little a host family experiences these reactions will depend somewhat on family members and how deeply they want to become immersed in learning experiences—experiences that can prompt quasi-culture shock reactions. Some may desire only a quick dip in and out. Others may feel challenged to take an extended plunge.

If you want to temper or slow down the frequency of quasi-culture shock reactions, we suggest that you mention to your exchange student that you prefer not to discuss sensitive topics or debate cultural differences for awhile. Also, try to schedule a lot of shared activities (trips to museums, craft fairs, sports events, special celebrations, etc.) and de-emphasize lengthy or deep discussions.

On the other hand, if a personal growth experience is what you want, you may find your house of mirrors exciting and the irreversible loss of cultural innocence enriching.

REWARDS FOR THE FAMILY

Host families frequently believe that the principal value in having an exchange student is the opportunity to share their home and lifestyle with someone from a distant land. As one family put it, "As Americans we have such abundance, so why not share it?" It was only after their student had returned home that this host family realized that something more and unexpected had happened, that they had been significantly changed by the experience. They had become more attuned to world issues, more mindful of their own enculturation, more cognizant of how people tend to "see" events from their own cultural perspective and more sensitive to the idea that each culture's way of life is equally valid. Heightened awareness and "dual vision" had dislodged them from being 100% Made-in-America.

People who share these kinds of broader cross-cultural perspectives and experiences constitute what might be called a "third culture." No longer immersed in a single culture, they are linked to a larger global community.

It is our hope that this book helps you relate to an exchange student in such a way that it serves as your passport into the third culture, enabling you to leave behind the security of the known and journey into new, exciting and challenging cross-cultural dimensions.

Like many families, you may be contemplating hosting a student for the first time, you may already have a student, or perhaps you're considering repeating the hosting experience. Why? Maybe you want to experience or re-experience the sense of deep accomplishment that comes from making a positive contribution to a youngster's development. Maybe you want to examine or re-examine your own values and lifestyle. Maybe you feel a longing to build a network of friendships around the globe. Or maybe, like the mother quoted below, you like the idea of becoming hooked on hosting:

The first time you try it and like it, you realize just how much you've been missing. So, of course, you want to do it again. It's like you've been led into a bountiful orchard of tempting juicy new experiences. You can't resist reaching for one more because the apples are just sitting there, ready for the picking.

PART II

Hosting Guidelines and Suggestions

7. Our Exchange Student Has Arrived

About now you may be saying to yourself that hosting an exchange student has the potential of being a meaningful and rewarding experience as well as a challenge. You might also feel that it would be helpful to have some practical hosting guidelines.

To provide this kind of practical guidance, we discuss in the next eight chapters the various stages of the hosting experience and examine some of the typical features of each. We will attempt to give you some idea about what to expect at different points in the homestay, and we will make recommendations on how to handle typical day-to-day situations.

The eight stages of hosting as portrayed in the diagram below are:

1 Arrival
2 Settling in
3 Deepening the relationship
4 Culture shock

5 The Holidays
6 Culture Learning
7 Pre-departure
8 Re-adjustment

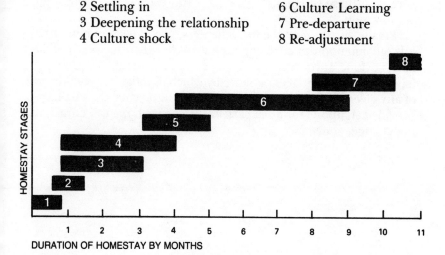

As you progress through the hosting experience, we hope that this framework will give added meaning and structure to events. If, at some point, you begin to suspect that adjustment roadblocks have developed—for either your student, family members or both—you might find it helpful to refer to our stages model to determine what may be causing difficulties. In situations such as this, try not to blame the student or conclude that you are an unfit host parent. Instead, talk the matter over and, if appropriate, seek constructive help from the sponsoring organization.

Remember, too, that the model we have developed will not describe every situation. All models are somewhat hypothetical, and there is little formal research available about the host family's experience. Also, each family and each student is unique. Furthermore, knowing that hosting experiences vary in length, we have somewhat arbitrarily chosen to base our model on a 10–month experience. If your student will be living with you for a shorter or longer period, you may find the stages somewhat condensed or expanded.

In particular, the eight-stage model may not apply to the following: brief homestays covering less than 16 weeks, "at-risk" students,[1] students who were initially with temporary families for extended periods, and students who have been moved to second or third host families. These special conditions go beyond the scope of this book but are briefly mentioned in the Postscript. For guidance with these situations, we suggest you consult the sponsoring organization.

Finally, as you read the next chapters, please keep in mind that it is our intention to offer suggestions rather than to specify what must be done. If you have previously hosted a student, you probably have your own special experience by which to judge the usefulness of any given suggestion. If you are new to the activity, then we have provided signposts for an experience which we hope will enrich, if not change, your life.

8. Stage One: Arrival

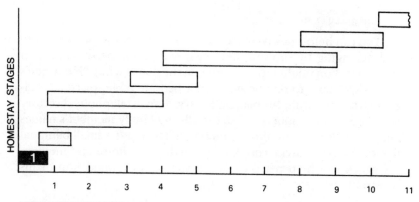

DURATION OF HOMESTAY BY MONTHS

Stage One begins the day an exchange student arrives[1] and usually ends before the one-month mark. Typically it lasts from seven to fourteen days.

When visitors arrive at the doorstep, we greet them enthusiastically to let them know they are welcome in our home. But for exchange students, coping with this initial period can be difficult. Not only may your student be confused by a handshake or misread your hugs and kisses (if this is not how greetings are expressed in his[2] own culture), but he may also be too weary with arrival fatigue to appreciate your expressions of hospitality.

Families often find that while their gestures of welcome may be overlooked and their words misunderstood, their concern for the student's adjustment is almost always appreciated. As one host mother notes:

> Of course I always smile and shake hands when I first meet our exchange students. But I try to put aside the idea that doing so means a whole lot. Instead, I do all I can to help that exhausted and confused kid regain his confidence and get his bearings. That's what's important. That's the best welcome.

Thus, without ever saying so in words, your thoughtful and comforting actions can convey to your student a message of welcome: "You're with people who understand what you're going through and who know how to be helpful."

To assist you with this kind of practical welcome, we've put together a number of suggestions which are designed to help bring a speedy recovery to arrival fatigue.

1. PERSONAL SPACE

You can help a newly-arrived student develop a sense of security and belonging by showing him what will be his personal area in the house. You might tape a banner on the door saying, "Henrique's room. Welcome to our house." On a bedside table, place a "Welcome Kit" containing air mail stationery; a small telephone directory with important numbers; a 3x5 card listing family member's names and your address and phone number; a housekey; a small bilingual dictionary. Also, invite your student to display photos and mementos which can help personalize the room and remind him of his cultural heritage.

2. SAFE ARRIVAL COMMUNIQUE

Contacting home within 24 hours of arrival is usually of primary importance. By so doing, students reassure both their natural family and themselves that all is well. They also re-establish an all-important bond with their parents,[3] and thus calm inner fears about being so far away. To reaffirm this bond, some students are content with sending a postcard with a brief "I'm here, and everything's fine" message. Others prefer to call collect. Either way, we strongly suggest you offer encouragement and assistance.

Also, if you haven't done so already, now is a good time to write a note to your student's parents. Briefly introduce your family, tell something about the way you live, and express your thanks for the opportunity to share their son or daughter.

3. JET LAG

Long international flights and layovers, combined with changes in time zones, weather, food and water, can leave a student exhausted. Encourage naps and expect irregular sleep and eating patterns. Ask about stomach upsets, especially diarrhea and constipation, and have medication available. Be supportive of your student's recuperation by pacing exposure to new experiences and minimizing overstimulation. Remember that initially a student's attention span may be short; plan welcoming parties and outings in accordance with signs of recovery.

You should also inquire about any prescription and non-prescription medication. (Sometimes this information is not included in the application papers.) With girls, ask if feminine hygiene products are needed, assist with their purchase, and clearly explain how to dispose of tampons and sanitary napkins. Also, you may eventually want to inquire about delayed menses since the stress of a cross-cultural adjustment frequently creates irregular patterns.

4. DECISIONS ABOUT NAMES

A decision needs to be reached regarding how your exchange student is to address you. Try to discuss this openly since what you're comfortable with could be awkward for the student. Some students and families reach a decision to use first names even though it is understood that the adults are more than peers. Others jointly decide that the adults are to be addressed as "Mom" and "Dad." If you opt for the latter, we suggest that it be clarified that you are not expecting the student to fit in like a son or daughter or adopt you as second parents.

Incidentally, some organizations strongly advise foreign students to automatically address their hosts as "Mom" and "Dad" and to relate to them as their parents. But our experience suggests that some students are extremely uncomfortable with that form of address. We think that discussing the matter first and reaching an understanding acceptable to both sides is best.

While discussing names, ask your exchange student if you are pronouncing his name correctly and if the name you're using is the one he prefers. If your student's name is difficult for Americans to pronounce, develop a phonetic pronunciation and write it on a card which can be shown to people. An example is: Caio (Ky' you); rhymes with "my you."

Sometimes families like to give their student an American name or nickname either because the student's real name is difficult to pronounce or because this is their way of expressing affection and inclusion. If you wish to do this, again we suggest you discuss the matter with your student. Some students feel that calling them by a new name is an insult or a threat to their identity. Others feel flattered by the attention.

5. LANGUAGE FATIGUE

Keep in mind that despite years of classroom language training, speaking English continuously can be nerve-wracking and exhausting for a newly-arrived student. To make matters worse, many students notice a decline in fluency during this stressful period. So try to minimize lengthy and complex discussions that may tax the student's fluency.

Consider creative solutions to communication barriers: draw pictures; try acting out what you want to say; and post signs around the house to label items like "oven," "hair dryer," etc.

During these first weeks, students make dozens of language errors. We suggest you ignore all but those which are likely to get the student in trouble or laughed at.[4] Similarly, since comprehension may be low, introduce at this time only major family rules and procedures.

6. MEALTIME

Bear in mind that table manners and food preferences vary from culture to culture. Be sensitive to food that the student might avoid for religious reasons and explain the mealtime customs that exist in the U.S. and in your household. When food is passed around the table, encourage family members to go first so that the student can observe what is the appropriate portion and how foods are eaten. If at first the student does not participate wholeheartedly in mealtime conversations, remember that speaking in English can be stressful. Also, some cultures do not encourage conversations during meals.

7. FAMILY INVOLVEMENT

If family members have household responsibilities, then one way to help the student begin to feel included is to assign some tasks to the student as well. However, it's best to start with a small assignment that can be easily explained and easily accomplished. An example might be asking the student to bring in the morning newspaper.

8. ORIENTATION

We suggest that soon after your student arrives, you give him a general tour of your home; even providing a simple map of the floor plan can be helpful. Initially, focus on areas he will use, taking care to ask whether he needs to be shown how things work, since toilets, showers, faucets and appliances sometimes function differently in other countries.

In a central place, post the family's schedule. Indicate when meals are served, when people get up, and the times of evening curfews, etc. By referring to this schedule, a student can gain a sense of when things will be happening.

During these first days, teach your student how to use the telephone and explain your family's system of receiving messages for others. (More comment on phone calls is provided in Chapters 10 and 11.)

During the first couple of weeks, introduce your student to important places in the community. But experienced host parents say it's best to go slowly; they try not to visit more than one place per day. On one of the first excursions, show your student how to get from your house to the local post office since students make frequent trips for postage and mailings. The next day, help the student set up a checking account at a local bank. In addition, help him become familiar with U.S. currency and give him an idea of what $1, $5, etc., will buy. On the following day, visit a nearby drugstore for purchases of such things as film, cosmetics, and other small items. In addition, students enjoy learning where the neighborhood library is and find it helpful to check out books about their country in order to explain things to Americans.

Plan to help the student with registration for classes (school enrollment should be pre-arranged by the sponsoring organization). Some schools[5] require that exchange students take certain prescribed courses. But when the choice is up to the student, some families encourage enrollment in classes like journalism, chorus, current events, etc., where there is more opportunity for conversing and making friends.

Schools usually have policies stating whether foreign students can participate in varsity sports, receive a diploma or hold senior standing. Many give students a class ring and yearbook, grant an honorary diploma or certificate of attendance and invite them to take part in graduation ceremonies even though requirements for graduation have not been met. In any case, get clarification on these matters so the student does not develop false expectations.

For your student's first days of school, try to find an American student (possibly your own son or daughter), who is willing to act as a guide—helping him get to the right bus, find classes, figure out how to work the lockers, make it through the cafeteria line, etc. (For more information about American high schools and the teenage subculture, see Chapter 10.)

9. Stage Two: Settling In

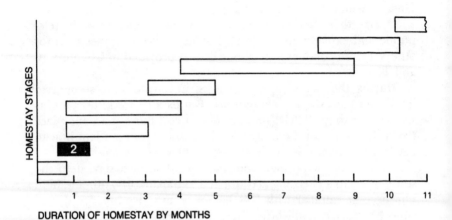

DURATION OF HOMESTAY BY MONTHS

Stage Two begins as early as the second week and can extend to the seventh week. Typically, it covers a five-week period.

As the student's arrival fatigue fades, you will probably want to spend time developing a compatible living arrangement. In the process, there may be some unpleasant "letdown" feelings as minor difficulties arise and reality sets in.[1] One host father aptly caught the spirit of Stage Two when he explained that a host family should expect to feel some discomfort. "Things will be going just right," he suggested, "when they start going a tad wrong!" A good adjustment has its rough spots for both the host family and the student.

On the pages that follow, three "settling in" experiences, which were reported by families that we interviewed, are described: 1) disruption of familiar family routines; 2) seeing imperfections in your exchange student; and 3) giving up romanticized expectations. In each section, there are ideas about what to expect and suggestions about what you can do to minimize the discomfort associated with things "going a tad wrong."

DISRUPTION OF FAMILIAR FAMILY ROUTINES

For a while, a break from life's routines and uneventful ruts can be a refreshing relief. But as any vacationer can tell you, all too soon we tire of mountain top highs and unending new vistas. Eventually we pack our suitcases and head home for the predictable, familiar and comfortable grooves of daily life.

So it is with host families. After two or three weeks of nonstop excitement, many begin to cool toward their exchange student and the hosting experience. They find that bringing an exchange student into the home has also brought disruptions. And worse, the disruptions have extended beyond the pleasure of a vacation. Not surprisingly, the family longs for a return to times that were more familiar and comfortable.

How might some of these disruptions be experienced? For starters, you will find that another person is tying up the bathroom and another person's T.V. preferences have to be considered; there are new concerns about privacy, semi-nudity and displays of affection; there's someone else competing for telephone time; another person is making midnight raids on the refrigerator; and additional teenagers and neighbors are stopping by for impromptu visits.

With all these changes, families may grow weary of the once dazzling international person living in their midst. One host mother expressed her shift in feelings this way:

> When Pascal arrived, he just walked in and sat down in our hearts. We thought, "Oh! This is just the perfect match." Now nothing seems to be matching.

As with this host parent, losing your "at-home" feeling may cause you to react with disappointment—even irritation and resentment—despite the fact that you fundamentally like the idea of having an exchange student.

Your children might have some reactions, too. They'll probably understand that an exchange student needs extra attention, but this also means there's less time for them. In addition, any loss of privacy might be resented (especially if a bedroom or study area is shared), and sometimes there's uneasiness about all the attention that friends and relatives shower on an exchange student. When these disturbances and losses occur, your children may react in ways that typically express insecurity: with feelings of jealousy, possessiveness and rivalry.

Unfortunately, the disruption of your familiar routines is something you can't do much about and for some families may not even be very significant. But if you are bothered by these changes, you can begin to regain comfortable "at-home" feelings by developing new patterns and adapting old routines. Bear in mind that your student will at the same time be trying to adjust to your routines and searching for her "niche" in the family. Here are some suggestions that may be helpful:

1. POSTPONE NEW PROJECTS

Try to avoid introducing additional disruptions at this time. For example, if you're thinking of re-carpeting the family room or building a sun deck, try to postpone the project for a few months. Adding additional disruptions can heighten or extend the period of irritability.

2. DEVISE NEW ROUTINES

With each routine that has been disrupted, jointly discuss the accommodations that can be made. Try not to accept a casual solution like, "Hey we've got a morning traffic jam in the bathroom. Everyone's got to get in and out faster!" Instead, work out a specific solution, like a detailed schedule designating a particular time for each person. Another solution might involve scheduling some showers for the evening.

While working out satisfactory new routines, encourage all family members—as well as your student—to be flexible and willing to compromise.

3. EXPECT SOME IRRITABILITY AND RESENTMENT

Help your children understand that feeling irritable is normal when family routines are disrupted. At the same time, help them understand that their irritation is with the changes and not with the exchange student.

Try to accept any feelings of jealousy and resentment. Even though your love for your children has not diminished, the time you have available to share with them probably has. While showing respect for your children's feelings, help them understand that lifestyle sharing involves both losing and gaining. Perhaps with your help, they can make a list of both the rewards and the hassles.

4. REMEMBER: DISRUPTIONS ARE TEMPORARY

Try to keep in mind that some disruptions are inevitable but not permanent. After about three to six weeks, you and your family should begin to feel a returning sense of comfort with daily routines.

NOTICING IMPERFECTIONS

Before an exchange student arrives, host families generally don't know much about the person with whom they will share their life and home. They might have an application form, a few facts from the sponsoring agency and a photo, often blurred. But that's about all.

In the absence of complete information, families sometimes start an embroidery process by mentally creating an exchange student who is perfect in almost every respect. These embroidered "dream students"—fictitious as they may be—often come in handy during the first awkward days and weeks. That's because when little is known and communication is strained, embellishments can serve as a kind of comforting substitute for real-world knowledge.

Although many families have fairly realistic expectations, it is not uncommon for families to romanticize a bit. How will you know if you are a host who has fashioned some version of a "dream student" in your mind?

Typically, "dream students" are expected to be flawless beings without bothersome imperfections and human blemishes. Some host parents try to turn their own untidy and grumpy children into angels by pointing to their newly-arrived "dream student" as a model of perfection with inbred happiness, like the spunky and sparkling kids in a Dr. Pepper commercial. There is even an occasional host parent who anticipates that a "dream student" will serve to make up for the teenage experiences he or she never had. This means the student is expected to be one of those super kids who wins all the awards at school assemblies and sets the pace for the popular crowd.

As first-hand information accumulates, it usually turns out that the student doesn't have a halo and is not a carbon copy of perfection. With this awareness can come a "letdown" sensation and the realization that all that colorful mental stitchery has outworn its purpose. One host mother who divested her student of this halo discovered that ordinary and unexceptional exchange students can offer friendship, caring and new ideas:

> I think families eventually have to accept that hosting is not going to be a wish fulfillment. Exchange students are not perfect and angelic like Hummel figurines. They're normal, ordinary kids who make mistakes, break things, hurt your feelings, get upset and say things in funny ways—just like your own kids.

Fantasies are a lot of fun but a fantasy won't teach you anything new, and it definitely can't give you a hug when you've had a terrible day.

If you happen to have some unrealistic expectations that need shedding, we suggest the following:

1. ACCEPT DISAPPOINTMENT

Bear in mind that you may go through the kind of "letdown" feelings that we have described. If you do, remember that these kinds of feelings are the result of your own expectations and not your student's fault.

2. DISCOVER TRUE FRIENDSHIP

Remember that your disappointment is only temporary. As it fades, you will be ready to discover the real similarities and differences between you and your exchange student. We think that it's these real-life discoveries that lead to true friendship.

SETTING REALISTIC GOALS

Along with developing an accurate image of their exchange student, it is also important that families consider the goals they might have for the hosting experience. People almost always set goals (which in turn create expectations) when they want to accomplish something. Even with something so routine as our morning shower, we want to come out feeling clean and invigorated. But what if we enter the shower hoping the pounding spray will enlarge our biceps? Then, no matter how clean and invigorated we become, we're likely to walk away feeling somewhat like a failure—or at least disappointed.

This example demonstrates the importance of setting realistic goals so that you give yourself the greatest possible chance of ending up satisfied and feeling successful. In previous chapters, we've described some of the hosting goals that we think are attainable: 1) taking an exchange student for the purpose of lifestyle sharing; 2) entering the experience with the goal of learning about cultures (your own and others); and 3) becoming host parents with the hope of developing a friendship with a person from another culture. Here's what one family says about their expectations:

When we took our first exchange student, we didn't give much thought to what we wanted to get out of it. Our neighbors did it, so why not give it a try?

Now we go into it with clear expectations, and it's something we discuss. We tell our student: "We've invited you here to show you American life, but we are also doing this for our own personal enjoyment, our own learning. And, if from all this, there's increased international understanding and peace in the world—now that's a nice bonus!"

We've seen families take a student to save their marriage, to provide a friend for their shy daughter, to get a live-in babysitter, to teach religion or to sell democracy. When students are taken for these kinds of reasons, the family can be programming itself for failure.

If you haven't already done so, perhaps now is a good time to think through what you hope to gain from the hosting experience. Talk with other experienced host families about their expectations and discuss with them whether or not your goals seem attainable. You might also consider the following:

1. COMPARE GOALS WITHIN THE FAMILY

Compare your particular expectations with those of other family members. Make note of the differences and try to accept the fact that everyone may not hold the same expectations. You might learn, for example, that your son isn't interested in developing as close a relationship with your exchange student as you are. This information can help you be more tolerant of him if he chooses not to spend a great deal of time with the student.

2. LIST YOUR REASONS

Take a piece of paper and actually write down all of the reasons you have for taking an exchange student. Invite other family members to do the same and then discuss the results.

3. DISCARD INAPPROPRIATE GOALS

During the process of sorting out their expectations, host families sometimes discover that certain goals can be better met in other ways. For example, someone who has taken an exchange student primarily to learn a foreign language might decide that the student can't really provide language instruction. Perhaps a better way to proceed is to enroll in a language class.

10. Stage Three: Deepening the Relationship

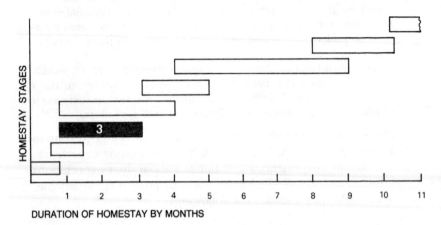

DURATION OF HOMESTAY BY MONTHS

Stage Three begins at approximately the one-month mark and continues until around the middle of the third month. Typically it covers about ten weeks.

During the early weeks of the homestay experience, host families aren't the only ones who have to grapple with unrealistic expectations. Exchange students can experience the same disillusionment when they realize: 1) that they might not have the perfect Hollywood family; 2) that to have a meaningful sojourn they must take the initiative to make it work—their U.S. experience will not just be "handed to them;" or 3) that adjustment has its unpleasant moments.

Eventually, students begin to involve themselves actively in the family's lifestyle. But it's uncommon for the shift from "waiting" to "actively participating" to happen overnight. For several days or weeks, students typically waver with thoughts like these:

> Is this where I'm going to stay, where I'm going to live for the next eight months? There are things I like about this family but things I don't. Can I tolerate what I don't like? If so, what must I do to make this a good experience?

Although it is essentially up to the exchange student to shift to full participation, the host family can do important things to assist.

You can begin by involving your student at deeper levels. We mentioned earlier that it's a good idea to discuss only essential rules when a student first arrives. Now we suggest you: 1) explain more thoroughly your family's rules and customs; 2) talk about the home-stay experience in substantive discussion; and 3) be as responsive as you can to the common concerns of this period.

None of these three tasks is simple. You may cringe at the thought of bringing up rules, "I'll be seen as an ogre. And, if we, get into serious talks, awful things could be said which will mar the nice experience we are having!" One host father who had these kinds of worries explains how and why he made the decision to move ahead:

> About six weeks into the hosting experience you realize: "Hey, if we want our exchange student to really understand our lifestyle, we've got to *make* it understandable. And, if we really want this person to be important to us, we've got to talk about the things that we actually *do* consider important.
>
> You just come to a dead end and realize you can't continue on as before. You have to turn the corner and say: "I'm going to do whatever it takes to make this a real-life, person-to-person adventure."

To help with turning the corner, we've put together some suggestions on how you as a host can present family rules, initiate heart-to-heart talks and deal with some common concerns.

RULES

Discussions about family rules serve as one of the major ways—if not *the* major way—that an exchange student learns what appropriate behavior is in your household. This is so important for your student's adjustment that we suggest you begin by scheduling informal weekly talks. At each meeting, try to focus on just a few rules so that the amount of information your student is asked to learn is manageable.

1. MAKE DISCUSSIONS A "LEARNING EXPERIENCE"

Try to approach the discussions as learning experiences rather than as lectures about what is "right and wrong." For example, while explaining one of your family's rules, invite your exchange student to describe how his family handles a comparable situation. In addition, discuss rules in terms of what they reflect about each culture's beliefs and standards. (Chapter 4 contains examples of situations that occur because of different cultural standards.) This can help your student gain an understanding that goes beyond lifestyle sharing to the broader dimension of culture learning. It also emphasizes the idea that learning and sharing are two-way processes.

Incidentally, when host families express a genuine interest in other cultures, students are often more comfortable conforming to their hosts' way of life.

2. SOME CUSTOM-MADE RULES MAY BE NECESSARY

In most cases, the rules for your own children will also be appropriate for an exchange student, especially if you have teenagers. But occasionally, separate rules make sense. For example, if your own children are ages 11 and 15, and the exchange student is 17, then a different curfew is appropriate. When developing custom-made rules, base your decisions on the student's level of maturity and experience. Then explain to your own children that different situations require different responses; the important thing regarding rules is that they be fair, not necessarily uniform.

3. EXPLAIN RULES THOROUGHLY

Family rules are generally so well understood that parents need only give their children brief reminders of what is expected. But a brief reminder isn't enough for an exchange student who comes from a different family with rules of its own. Consequently, it is important that you not understate the rules that you expect your student to follow.

An example of an understated rule is: "If you're not coming home after school, call." A more specific and exact version is: "If you're not planning to be home from school by 4 o'clock, call home and let us know your plans."

4. WATCH FOR OVERPROTECTIVENESS

Most host families view being in charge of someone else's teenager as an important responsibility. Sometimes their concern causes them to become overprotective and impose restrictions that are too severe. If you sense this may be happening, try to ease up a bit. Aim for policies that are in line with the student's age, experiences and level of maturity.

5. RECOGNIZE THE DIFFERENCE BETWEEN SPOKEN
AND UNSPOKEN RULES

Many family rules are spoken rules—rules that parents verbally explain and actively enforce. "Only one hour of T.V. on school nights," might be the rule in one family. Another family might not say anything about how long the T.V. is watched but will insist on, "No snacks before dinner" or "Only 15 minutes per phone call." Some families try to keep rules to a minimum and say: "We have only two rules: Be honest and show consideration to other family members. For everything else, use your own judgment." But regardless of the number of spoken rules, family members can usually recite them, and they know the consequences if the rules are broken.

What we seldom realize is that the majority of our family patterns are governed by unspoken rules and expectations that are rarely discussed or even thought about. These silent rules are frequently a reflection of culturally-based assumptions about what appropriate behavior is, and they constantly influence our thinking and actions. Examples are: "Family members should always volunteer to help each other and not wait to be asked," "When upset, girls in the family can cry; boys are allowed to get angry and occasionally swear," "Never eat the last piece of cake without first offering to share it," "If Dad falls asleep while watching T.V., don't change the channel!"

Among the culturally-based unspoken rules, there are certain topics that almost all host families need to discuss. Otherwise, students and their families often reach wrong conclusions. These topics include: 1) How we express appreciation/thanks in our family; 2) How we express disagreement; 3) What does it mean in our family to be "on time"; 4) What's private property and what belongs to the family as a whole; 5) When and where (in the house) can teenagers entertain their friends. (For example, many European teens entertain in their bedrooms. Is that O.K. in your home?); 6) The meaning of a shut and/or locked bedroom door (I'm angry, I'm resting, Don't bother me, I'm thinking); 7) appropriate bathroom etiquette and hygiene.[1]

These matters need to be discussed so that both the student and the family can be sensitive to each other and so that agreed upon behavior patterns are established. Also bear in mind that sorting out cultural differences often takes considerable time and patience because so many subtle and/or confusing factors can interfere with the clarification process.

6. TENSION MAY SIGNIFY THAT AN UNSPOKEN
RULE HAS BEEN BROKEN

When unspoken rules are are not followed, we may sense that something is wrong but can't say exactly what. We just have an uneasy feeling that all is not well. Try to watch for this uneasy feeling, and, when you can, identify the unspoken rule that has been violated. Then explain the situation to your student, trying whenever possible to include discussions about unspoken cultural assumptions, values and perceptions.

7. BE PATIENT: LEARNING RULES TAKES TIME

Even though your student may be completely committed to adapting to life in your household, it is not an easy task. And it takes time. How long will depend on numerous factors. With guidance, a student should be able to adjust to the spoken rules in four to six weeks. Developing an understanding of the unspoken rules in both the family and the culture at large will, in many cases, takes much longer. Patience is called for.

HEART-TO-HEART TALKS

Discussing rules is necessary and can often be quite revealing, but it's also important to open lines of deeper communication. This can be done through serious discussions, or heart-to-heart talks. As much as possible, these should be discussions in which thoughts may be freely shared and feelings of happiness and displeasure expressed. It is especially important during the first weeks and months to carefully clarify what living with your family is going to be like.

Some families find that the dinner table is an ideal setting for these discussions. Others set aside a special time. However you choose to arrange it, we hope you will get in the habit of talking often and openly. Described below are several topics that are good to consider:

1. VOICE YOUR ACCEPTANCE OF THE STUDENT

Because the early weeks of the homestay are often filled with commotion and sparse communication, families sometimes forget to tell exchange students they are indeed wanted and accepted. Or, families sometimes express their caring in ways that are misunderstood by the student.

For example, one student began tensing up with stomach cramps before meals because his refusal to sample new foods or take second helpings was interpreted by the family as a rejection of their hospitality. If as a host you find yourself tempted to "bake someone happy," explain that Americans often use food to express how much they like another person. Then state verbally (rather than through food) that the student is welcome and wanted.

2. DESCRIBE YOUR FAMILY IN UNEXCEPTIONAL TERMS

One of the major areas of discussion should be the family itself. As a host, you may need to remind your student repeatedly that he has come to live with ordinary earthlings whose lives are filled with unexceptional, every-day experiences; in other words, help your student develop a realistic concept of your family and the life you lead. Point out what is normal and typical in your day-to-day living and clarify what you anticipate will make the homestay experience special within the context of real-life possibilities. For example, explain to your student that a large part of this experience will consist of sharing pretty average, daily events which you anticipate will lead to an exciting exchange of ideas and learning.

3. EXPLAIN WHAT IT MEANS
TO PARTICIPATE IN SOMEONE'S LIFESTYLE

As you involve the student in your lifestyle, clarify what "involvement" actually means. Explain that although you want him to try living like an American, you are not asking him to renounce his own culture and in effect become "Americanized." Point out that involvement means: 1) experimenting with and sampling U.S. ways of doing things; 2) learning *why* Americans do some of the things they do; 3) developing an understanding of your way of life and how it is shaped by American culture; and 4) learning the rules and skills necessary to participate in your family and American culture as fully as possible.

4. EXPLAIN THE MEANING OF CHORES

Another topic to discuss is family chores. If you're like most Americans, everyone in the household is expected to help with the upkeep of the home and everyone has been assigned specific chores. Because you want your exchange student to participate fully in your home, you'll want to assign him chores too. But before you do, explain the following: 1) It is customary in U.S. families to pitch in and help with the housekeeping rather than employ housekeepers; 2) many American parents believe household responsibilities have an important influence on the development of character in that chores help build traits of responsibility, dependability and thoroughness.

In other cultures, parents often have totally different ways of fostering maturity, so your student may not approach chores with a great deal of seriousness. With this in mind, you might assign your student some household task for the purpose of giving him the opportunity to experience an American custom rather than for the purpose of developing or testing maturity.

While explaining your family's view of household chores, ask your student to describe his family's procedures for maintaining the home and how his parents have helped with his character development. In some cases, students explain that their sojourn to the U.S. is their parents' way of fostering independent decision-making and broadened horizons.

5. TALK ABOUT POSSIBLE FEELINGS OF INDEBTEDNESS

Occasionally students are uncomfortable knowing that families generally receive no compensation for hosting. Feeling indebted for what is being done in their behalf, some students begin to believe they must repay the family's kindness by never complaining, constantly looking happy, always putting their hosts' wants before their own, etc. But this kind of guilt-motivated "good behavior" can keep a student from being a "normal" human being and may lead to smoldering resentment.

To counter this tendency, make it clear to your student that he is welcome to express his opinions freely, to have his own likes and dislikes, to say "no" when he needs to and to make mistakes.

COMMON CONCERNS

1. LANGUAGE PROBLEMS

Because many students have difficulty communicating in English, any help you can provide will probably be greatly appreciated. Even students who have studied English for many years make pronunciation mistakes or use American slang in inappropriate ways. For example, a Greek boy startled his host mother when he remarked, "We don't eat snakes in Greece like you do in the U.S."

What brought about the mother's alarm was a mere language error—the boy had mispronounced the word "snacks." Similarly, a Swedish girl gave her host family a chuckle when she explained, "In my country it's not customary to smell (smile) in pictures." While such mistakes often seem amusing to native speakers, the experience for your exchange student might be a painful one.

To help your student develop greater fluency in English, there are some things you can do: 1) encourage him to carry a small bilingual dictionary (or phrase book); 2) help him develop a curiosity for language by discussing the meaning of words and by helping him understand colorful expressions; 3) even though it may take your student a long time to compose his thoughts in English, be very patient and try not to interrupt him, finish his sentences for him or second-guess his answers; 4) speak simply (but not simple-mindedly; your student is no doubt quite intelligent) and resist the temptation to solve communication problems by raising your voice—poor hearing is rarely the cause; 5) if your student's fluency is extremely low, ask the sponsoring organization if tutoring services are provided. (For additional language-learning aids, see Appendix A.)

2. MONEY ISSUES

The concerns that pertain to money can for the most part be grouped under one of the following four headings: wealthy students, spendthrifts, trips and weekly allowances.

Wealthy Students. Exchange students who come from affluent, highly-educated and well-traveled families may have difficulty adjusting to life in a middle-income American home. The student might not realize that spending money at a breezy clip can create discomfort for his host family. Conversely, the family may have difficulty being sensitive to the adjustment problems faced by a youngster who is used to a "privileged" life. If this becomes a problem, discuss the differences with the student. Try to develop an appreciation for his experience and ask him to try to accept any limitations that come from sharing your family's middleclass style of living.

Spendthrifts. Frequently students arrive with ample spending money but lack an understanding of how much their American dollars will buy, or they become "addicted" to U.S. gadgetry and begin buying everything in sight! An unfortunate result is that some students run out of money by Christmas—just when they need to be buying winter clothes. One way of preventing this from happening is to help your student budget his money. But don't be too strict. Many students will want to buy gifts to take home. Money for such purchases shouldn't be included in a budget for routine expenses.

Trips. Most programs require that students provide their own spending money. But for special trips and dining out, problems can arise because neither the student nor the family is quite sure who should pay.

We suggest that with some advance planning this potentially thorny problem can be avoided. Discuss with your student what you will be doing and how you want to share the expenses involved. Sometimes families are comfortable paying when the whole family goes out for special dinners or weekend trips. Other times they ask the student to pay half or all of his own "special-occasion" expenses.

You may find it unpleasant to talk about such matters, but it seems there is no painless alternative. When a family is reluctant to pay but avoids talking about it, resentments and misunderstandings can result.

Weekly Allowance. Some families decide to give their exchange student an allowance, although many do not. What's important is that the exchange student have roughly the same amount of spending money as other teenagers in the family and/or the school community. If your student comes from a wealthy family, explain that having and spending a lot of money while living in your home will make him an outsider to your lifestyle. Once this has been understood, it's important to write to the student's natural parents and request that a controlled allowance procedure be established.

3. PHONE CALLS

Being an exchange student often means the loss of some privileges. For example, most students are not allowed to drive a car in the U.S., so they sometimes latch on to the telephone as a substitute way of socializing. But since phone calls can be expensive (especially when exchange students call other exchange students who live in another part of the country), it's good to establish procedures regarding usage and payments.

Sometimes families worry that their exchange student will not make a good adjustment unless all phone contact with the natural parents is severed. And some sponsoring organizations stipulate that phone calls home are to be actively discouraged. Calls home are important for most teenagers living away from their natural families, but students should not be encouraged to use calls home as a substitute for working out adjustment concerns. Good sense should be the guide here. Some continued contact with natural families is probably conducive to a good adjustment. But if phone calls home increase in length and frequency, it may be a signal that problems have developed—in which case family discussions and/or counseling may be advised so that the student's adjustment can be facilitated and phone contact gradually diminished.

Regarding procedures for handling the expense of phone calls, many families ask their students to: 1) call collect when making overseas calls; and 2) use pay phones when calling long distance in the U.S. These procedures may sound heartless, but imagine receiving a phone bill for $600! "Don't worry," your student might reassure you. "I'll give you the money when I get a check from home." Meanwhile, the days roll by and the phone company starts sending reminders.

4. SCHOOL ADJUSTMENT

Contending with school and the teenage subculture can be one of the biggest hurdles an exchange student encounters. He may have a difficult time understanding classroom lectures, be dazed by the frantic pace of students dashing madly from class to class every 50 minutes, feel threatened by the peer pressure to experiment with alcohol, sex and drugs, and find confusing the importance placed on extracurricular activities.

It is often quite difficult for foreign students to understand what is considered appropriate classroom behavior. Many students come from cultures where the relationship with teachers is more formal, where competition and emphasis on individual effort is less evident, where little or no discussion occurs in the classroom, where definitions of cheating and plagarism are different from our own or where homework is nonexistent. Before an exchange student can comfortably conform to U.S. high school norms, these matters may need to be discussed at length.

To help, you might: 1) encourage your student to make friends with American youths,[2] but be sympathetic to the frustrations he may encounter along the way; 2) help him find a "guide"—an adolescent who will help him learn the spoken and unspoken rules for getting along with American teenagers; 3) de-emphasize high scholastic performance so that it does not add to the stresses already present; 4) introduce yourself to his teachers and keep abreast of his progress; 5) find a teacher who takes a special interest in foreign students (perhaps a language or social studies teacher who might be willing to involve your student in cross-cultural activities or at least check on his adjustment from time to time).

Lest you fear that you'll never learn or be able to remember everything we've described in this chapter, take a deep breath and relax. There's not a student anywhere who will bring with-him all of the common concerns we've described. But if and when a concern emerges, you now have some background information to help you identify and resolve it. With enough patience and understanding, we hope you'll be rewarded with a farewell note similar to the one which a departing student left for his family:

> . . . There were some ups and downs, but we managed to solve all the problems [and] I really appreciate all the things you and your family did for me. . .
>
> I love you, but I can't find the words to say it. Maybe someday I will have the words to describe my feelings. A big part of me will remain here. I will love you always.

11. Stage Four: Culture Shock

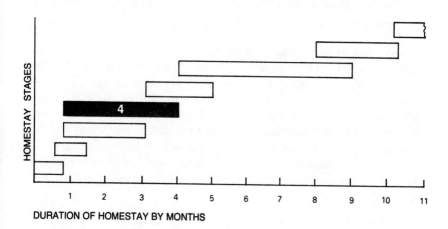

HOMESTAY STAGES

4

1 2 3 4 5 6 7 8 9 10 11

DURATION OF HOMESTAY BY MONTHS

The culture shock stage begins roughly at the end of the first month and extends until the fourth month. Generally, it covers a three-month period. This stage somewhat overlaps in time with the previous stage.

As household rules are clarified and more substantive discussions initiated, exchange students begin to feel involved with their host families. At the same time, learning about another way of life makes it clear that there are innumerable confusing differences which distinguish one culture from another.

As we suggested in earlier chapters, culture shock is a real and sometimes disruptive result of encountering those differences.[1] But how will you know when it happens? Seasoned host families report that a student experiencing culture shock might:

Dread going to school because classmates are "arrogant" and the U.S. educational system is "disgusting."

Lash out in anger because of an innocent remark at the dinner table; or make a retreat to the bedroom where crying goes on for hours.

Long for family and friends back home who "really understand."

Withdraw at times, become irritable, ignore rules or exhibit unusual shyness.

Describe confusing or threatening situations as "stupid" or "dumb."

Complain about feeling unloved or unjustly criticized.

Escalate minor squabbles with other family members into standoffs.

Find it difficult to hold normal conversations.

There may even be times when students feel enormously threatened, especially if they find that conforming to their host's lifestyle requires that they go against cherished personal values. This was the experience of Leena, a Finnish student who became quite anxious when she accompanied her host family to church each Sunday morning. Church attendance was central to her host's way of life but very foreign to Leena, who was not religious. To Leena, participating in church services caused her to experience a discrepancy between what she believed and how she was behaving. She describes the insecurity she felt:

> I would go to the parish with my family because this was a big part of their life. But I felt very funny dressing up and going to church. I would sit there singing songs that meant nothing to me and saying amen to statements I didn't believe in. I felt like a hypocrite who was living one big lie. Each Sunday I would sit there wondering, "Who am I, and what am I doing here?"

Perhaps the most common symptom of culture shock is the inability to hold a normal conversation. Of course, there are a number of reasons why a student may be uncommunicative, but many otherwise friendly and intelligent students lose their ability to converse freely while going through culture shock. One reason for this is that too much of a student's attention is diverted away from day-to-day interactions while she is contending with a massive, internal unscrambling process; learning about a new culture can be like trying to put together two gigantic jigsaw puzzles (one representing your culture, the other your student's) whose pieces have become thoroughly intermingled. With this kind of a challenge, a student may at times appear tuned out, illogical and closed-minded. "When culture shock would wash over me," one student said, "it felt like my mind had been erased."

Frequently, families find it hard to know how to comfort and guide a student through culture shock. That's because, as hard as one may try, it is often extremely difficult to acknowledge and understand culture shock for what it is. And because you probably want your student to have a positive, happy experience, you may want to coax her out of culture shock reactions or pretend they don't exist. Here's how a host mother describes the disbelief that interfered with her ability to identify what her student was experiencing:

> When Juanita, our first exchange student, locked herself in her bedroom and cried all afternoon, wanted to sleep with the light on and complained that our food tasted like sawdust, I concluded that I wasn't being a good host.
>
> After all, house guests never cry or want to go home unless you treat them bad, right? So, I set out on this big campaign to pull her out of it. "Let's shower this kid with love and really get her involved," I told my husband. When that didn't work, I started scolding her: "If you really wanted to, you could feel good." You see, I was convinced Juanita was just being stubborn or disobedient or lazy. Culture shock? That's a bunch of bunk! I believed that if she really wanted to, Juanita could feel great, get involved at school and make lots of friends.
>
> And when that also failed to happen, I called the sponsoring organization and complained to them, saying they'd made a bad choice with Juanita. "She's not exchange student material. You didn't prepare her for this experience," I informed them. Through all of this, I just couldn't accept the reality of what culture shock does to a person.

For this host mother, several years passed and several exchange students had come and gone before she developed an indepth appreciation of culture shock; for her, the change was a gradual process that entailed going through a series of learning steps and developing new strengths and skills. Specifically, this involved: 1) recognizing her own feelings of disbelief; 2) developing a tolerance for the strong feelings experienced by her students; 3) noticing that most of her students went through similar unsettling experiences and concluding that culture shock reactions must be a normal part of living in a new culture; 4) realizing that in time, culture shock runs its course and the symptoms begin to fade; and 5) developing practical techniques for being of assistance. Commenting on her growth, this same host mother said:

> Now that I can tolerate culture shock in our exchange students, I'm freed up from being the rescuer; now I can empathize, give support and be of real help.

The following information can help you feel confident about relating to a student who is experiencing culture shock:

GENERAL SUGGESTIONS:

1. DEFINE WHAT IS HELPFUL

The way families respond to culture shock varies considerably from failing to provide any constructive help to being overly concerned and feeling guilty about distress that they didn't cause. To sort out the differences between appropriate and inappropriate help, we've compared helping a student with culture shock to helping a spouse with motion sickness.

If your spouse becomes dizzy, uncommunicative and complains of nausea during an airplane flight, it's unlikely that you'd conclude your mate is weak-willed, unsociable or a liar. Chances are, you would recognize his or her reactions as legitimate symptoms of motion sickness—a malady caused by the airplane's rolling and pitching. No doubt you would feel concerned about your loved one, but not to the extent of concluding that you were personally responsible for causing the unpleasant symptoms. And, if you were knowledgeable, you might suggest that your spouse reduce some of the discomfort by reclining in his or her seat. But at the same time, you would know that as long as the plane was aloft, there was no way you could personally end your spouse's motion sickness. In short, you would view the condition as real; you would not see yourself as responsible for either causing or ending the symptoms; and, if you knew how, you might want to provide some symptomatic relief.

In a similar sense, culture shock is a real condition caused by environmental changes over which you, as a host parent, have very little control: You are not responsible for having caused it; nor are you responsible for making it go away. The most you can do is provide temporary, symptomatic relief and minimize any additional stress factors.

2. DISCUSS CULTURE SHOCK BEHAVIOR

On days when your student feels comfortable talking, you might discuss the meaning of culture shock and point out the common ways that students typically experience it. Help her accept her own culture shock behavior as normal (sometimes students mistakenly believe that culture shock only happens to "weak-willed" or "immature" students). In these discussions, one host mother says the following to her student: "I understand there will be times when you feel bad. It's O.K. Sometimes talking about it helps the pain go away. So if you want to talk, I'm available." Another helpful message is this: "Culture shock is normal. If I were in your country, I'd be feeling just like you are."

3. ENCOURAGE "REACHING-OUT" BEHAVIOR

During the culture shock stage, it is important that a student find ways of reaching out to others. At first your student might only want to talk to you or another family member about what she is experiencing, or she may only share her thoughts with another exchange student. But as she experiences success with these initial efforts, she should be encouraged to find additional ways of reaching out. This might involve trying to make friends with a classmate, getting involved in some school activity, going to a movie with a neighbor, etc. In each instance, encourage her to move at a pace that is appropriate to her needs and personality and that can be handled successfully.

WAYS YOU CAN HELP EASE YOUR STUDENT'S DISTRESS

1. ALLOW FOR "TIME-OUT" PERIODS

Culture shock behavior is not a continuous thing; typically, it comes and goes. One day a student will be fine, the next day she may feel miserable. During periods of misery, it might be best if you refrain from deep or complicated discussions, refrain from teaching new customs or new household routines and refrain from introducing additional stress. You might want to think of these as "coasting" or "time-out" periods when communication and learning are postponed.

"Time-outs" are important because culture shock is an anxiety reaction to change, and people do not function well or think clearly when they are anxious. They tend, instead, to be argumentative and defensive; and if pressured, they can become defiant and panic-stricken.

When Leena (the Finnish girl who felt uneasy at church services) could not cope because of culture shock, her host family allowed her to stay home on Sundays. Given this "time-out," Leena's nervousness began to subside. Several months later, feeling more secure, she began to attend church services occasionally by her own choice.

2. EXPECT PERIODIC WITHDRAWAL

There are times when a student just doesn't want to be involved in much of anything and might withdraw temporarily. This may occur because she is feeling confused, mentally exhausted or homesick. Needing time to be alone, rest and think things through, she may retreat to her bedroom and lock the door. As one student stated, "In those moments I just needed my 'lonely time.' "

If, during these withdrawal periods, your student seems to be oblivious to your existence, try not to view this behavior as a sign of rejection. One host mother explained the situation well when she stated: "It's not that your student doesn't love you; it's that during this ordeal of culture shock, she simply can't."

3. EXPECT DISAGREEMENTS AND RESPOND TO THEM

If disagreements develop between your student and your children, try to minimize the amount of time they spend together. Then explain to your children that your exchange student may not have the strength, at present, to be a friend.

4. BE PREPARED FOR JUDGMENTAL REMARKS

If you find your student reacting to your ways of doing things with comments like, "That's stupid," or "How disgusting," it may help to: 1) remember that this is a culture shock reaction; the unspoken message is: "I can't cope"; 2) try not to get involved in a discussion since your student probably won't be open to your ideas; 3) try to be understanding and respond by saying something like, "It sounds like our custom doesn't make any sense to you," or, "I can see you are really disgusted and upset about this."

5. ENCOURAGE EXTRA REST

When things seem bewildering or threatening, as with Flávio, Leena and Axel, a student can begin to feel physically drained and need extra rest. One host parent explained that for several weeks her student came home from school, ate a small snack and then slept until dinnertime. "Jean-Jacques wasn't being lazy," she explained. "He needed the sleep to recuperate from the 'American high school maze.'"

6. DON'T CREATE "NO-EXIT" SITUATIONS

In addition to getting rest, students also need to find ways of strengthening their sense of cultural identity[2], which may be a bit shaky. For some students, a call home to loved ones during this period can be reassuring; for others, talks with another exchange student may be the answer, giving them the sense that the reactions which are upsetting them are understood and experienced by others. As one student explained it, "When I call my parents, they try to understand what I am going through, but sometimes they can't. When I speak with another exchange student, we understand. We speak the same 'hard times language.'"

To repeat what has been stated earlier, however, students should be discouraged from using the telephone as a substitute for coming to terms with issues central to adjustment. If you or the sponsoring organization questions the benefit of certain calls, try not to react with demands that have the effect of blocking phone contact suddenly and completely. Instead, discuss the matter openly with the student so that underlying issues can be clarified and changes gradually implemented.

The one thing we don't recommend during this period of upheaval is to give an ultimatum: "No more phone calls, period!" Doing so can create "no-exit" feelings of entrapment and panic since the calls may be perceived as vital lifeline. Such a decree can also seriously undermine rapport and trust, prompting the student to maintain the prohibited phone contact through secretive and devious means.

7. TOLERATE YOUR STUDENT'S INTENSE FEELINGS

After a phone call home or a chat with another exchange student, your student may seem more agitated than relieved. This frequently occurs because contacts with loved ones and co-nationals can stir up a variety of strong feelings: tenderness, loss, closeness, relief and joy. All these feelings may be expressed in an outpouring of tears. Although intense, such moments can be quite beneficial—easing your student's recovery. As one student stated, "I would have feelings jailed up inside of me. I had to liberate them. Crying was the best way. Afterwards, I got better."

8. MINIMIZE COMPLICATIONS

While your student is going through culture shock, she might experience considerable anxiety and depression. Just coping with simple things like getting up in the morning, being civil with the family or concentrating on homework assignments can require a lot of energy and seem like major accomplishments.

Because your student may already be coping at her maximum, try not to do things that could create additional stress. Increased stress might come from: 1) leaving the student alone for extended periods of time; 2) taking her on trips or to parties; 3) introducing her to relatives; 4) pressuring her to get high grades at school; 5) prohibiting her from calling home or talking to co-nationals; 6) pressuring her to recover quickly from culture shock; 7) teasing or joking about her strange culture shock behavior; 8) asking her to give talks or show slides of her country to large groups.

9. WARNING SIGNS THAT MAY SIGNAL THE NEED FOR PROFESSIONAL HELP

Described in this chapter and in Chapter 5 are the various normal culture shock reactions that a student may experience. These include: minor changes in appetite, moodiness and mild depression, increased smoking, minor changes in sleep patterns, occasional irritability or withdrawal, faultfinding or exaggerated praise of the host culture and homesickness. In the rare event that your student has extreme reactions over a prolonged period of time or becomes unusually disruptive, she may need professional help. Here are some of the behaviors that would signal a need for outside help: 1) excessive sleeping or insomnia; 2) significant weight gain or loss; 3) prolonged acute depression; 4) illegal behavior such as shoplifting, vandalism, etc.; 5) repeated use of alcohol or illicit drugs; 6) drastic decline in school grades or truancy; 7) excessive calls home or to co-nationals; 8) serious communication barriers with the host family; 9) suicidal tendencies and/or behavior.

If your student experiences one or more of the above reactions, it may be merely an indication of a very intense—though normal—culture shock reaction which will subside with time if special support is prescribed. On the other hand, there are times when an intense culture shock reaction may be a symptom of more fundamental problems. Sorting out the difference and recommending appropriate interventions should be left to professionals.

Should you desire more specific information about any of these behaviors or if you have concerns that your student's culture shock reactions may be extreme in nature, we suggest you seek clarification. The sponsoring organization's local representative is the first person to contact, and he or she should be able to put you in contact with professionals who have cross-cultural counseling expertise and can make professional assessments.

12. Stage Five: The Holidays

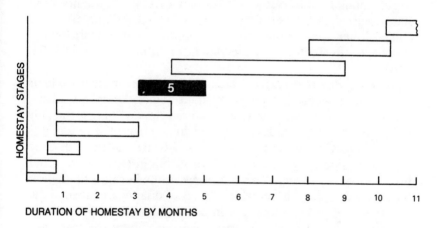

HOMESTAY STAGES

DURATION OF HOMESTAY BY MONTHS

Stage Five begins in the third month and can continue until the fifth month. Typically, however, it covers a six-week period centering on the Christmas holidays. If a student is not in the U.S. over the holidays, this stage will be skipped.

For many American families, the period between Thanksgiving and New Year's is a time of mistletoe and merrymaking. In both Jewish and Christian households, there is worship and celebration, special foods are prepared, religious vows are renewed, and annual visits from relatives are eagerly anticipated.

Knowing that the holiday season is a time of happiness with loved ones, host families often want to involve their students in their cherished customs and share with them a lively festive spirit. "We told Marcos that he'd find our Christmas season simply enchanting, and he did," enthused one host mother. "The day we took him caroling, he radiated like a neon sign."

In many cases, expectations for a cheery Christmas are totally fulfilled. But there are also times when the holidays turn out to be more stressful than joyous. Some students find themselves unable to participate in their family's celebrations because they have slipped back into a variation of culture shock which we call "the holiday blues."

What happens? With all of the talk about the magic of Christmas, students become preoccupied with memories of loved ones back home. Because thoughts are elsewhere and because host family traditions may not be familiar, it's even possible for a student to begin feeling like an "outsider." Then, particularly in the northern states, with winter days turning everything cold and grey like their chilled inner spirit, some students withdraw rather than involve themselves in lighthearted merriment or unfamiliar social situations.

The holiday blues affect about one out of every two students and typically result in a period of mild homesickness. For many, the need to call home or retreat for a brief "lonely" time is the only indication that the holidays have had some effect. For others it is more severe. One Norwegian girl was so adversely affected that she became frightened at the thought of giving gifts or meeting her hosts' relatives. During Christmas week, while her host family was humming carols and hoping for snow, Kari disappeared from sight. She retreated to her room, got in bed and bundled up in a huge protective mound of fluffy, warm blankets. There she remained for two days.

If the home Kari was in had been yours, you might have been quite surprised when she said she found it frightening to think about giving presents and visiting relatives. After all, aren't gift-giving and socializing enjoyed by everybody? "Good grief," you might have thought. "It never dawned on me that someone could experience our Christmas season as frightening." Next, you might correctly have concluded that Kari's strange behavior was an over-reaction—an expression of culture shock anxiety. And when she retreated to her bedroom, you might have responded by looking for ways you could help ease her distress.

But that's not what happened. Unfortunately, Kari's host family didn't realize that her behavior was a result of culture shock. Instead, her withdrawal was misinterpreted as rejection. Confused and feeling unwanted, the family failed to perceive Kari's real needs. Here's what the host mother said:

> When Kari retreated to her bedroom, something snapped inside of me. I sort of stepped sideways into a whole different way of behaving. It just happened to me like falling into a stage role. Feelings started boiling up, but I wasn't attuned to them. I reacted on reflex—dashing about being grouchy, feeling put upon and unloved. For two days I kept thinking, "What's wrong with that dumb kid? She's stomping on us! She's messing up our Christmas."
>
> Not once did I stop and think, "Hey, I've lost my objectivity. I need to get back to realistic thoughts and feelings." I had fallen into a different way of functioning and was taking everything personally.

By Christmas Eve, however, this host mother had partially regained her objectivity, recognizing that a communication breakdown existed and outside help was needed:

> Slowly I began to realize that Kari wasn't being mean or punishing; she was frightened and coping the only way she knew how. But still, I felt shut out. My feelings of rejection had gotten so high I just couldn't climb over them and be of help.
>
> So on Christmas Eve, I called a friend who agreed to be our moderator. Ana could see both sides. She helped Kari rejoin the family, and she helped me regain my objectivity.

What Kari and her host family had experienced was a breakdown in communication which occurred when both sides lost their ability to think clearly. The student had slipped into culture shock and the family was going through a brief period of quasi-culture shock. Although collisions like this don't occur with great frequency, even experienced host families report that they periodically face similar dilemmas.

Because you may find yourself at a collision point—either during the holiday season or at some other time during the homestay period—the following recommendations are provided:

1. PLAN AHEAD

Try to help your student be a part of your own festivities as well as his or her natural family's celebration. You might: 1) help see that cards and packages are mailed early so that they will reach the natural family in time for the holidays; 2) ask the student to prepare a favorite food or tell you about a custom from home that can be part of your activities here; 3) help find a good time to call home when international circuits aren't too busy.

2. BE PREPARED FOR UPSETTING EXPERIENCES

Keep in mind that during the holidays (or any other time), quasi-culture shock may be experienced by both first-time *and* experienced host families.

3. BE TOLERANT AND UNDERSTANDING

Understanding culture shock and the stages of adjustment can help "immunize" you against overreaction and loss of objectivity.

4. SEEK HELP IF SERIOUS DIFFICULTIES ARISE

If you begin to sense that you are in the midst of a communication impasse, you might want to bring in a moderator to help restore understanding. Be sure to choose someone who can be impartial and hear both sides clearly. People to consider might be: a school counselor, a minister or pastoral counselor, a cross-cultural counselor, a teacher or any professional who will not take sides.

13. Stage Six: Culture Learning

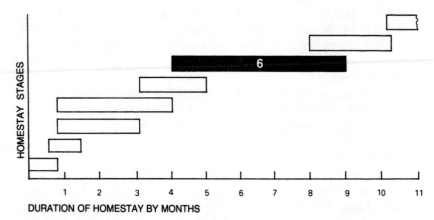

Stage Six begins in about the fourth month and extends through the eighth. Typically, it covers a four-month period.

"A friendship unfolds like a budding flower. Suddenly you have a gorgeous full bloom!" That's how one seasoned host father described his experience during this stage which tends to span the four-month period bounded by January and May. The families that we interviewed described this stage as the main attraction in the hosting experience. It's a time when the overall comfortable fit that has been achieved shows up in easy flowing but serious talk-a-thons, laughter, tender confidences, lighthearted teasing and comfortable silences.

But this upbeat experience may not be the norm.[1] If, by this point, a solid relationship has not been established, then the host and student may become disenchanted, adjustment can be hindered, and the motivation for problem-solving could be minimal. One official who supervises student placements offers the following explanation of what can happen:

> For perhaps the majority of host families, the period after Christmas is pleasant but fairly uneventful. But about 25 percent move into a very exciting phase of learning and for another 25 percent, the experience turns sour.
>
> For this latter group, the post-Christmas period is fraught with disappointment and mounting frustration. At some point, a complaint will be lodged by either the student or the family, and it will look like some specific incident suddenly has damaged their relationship.
>
> But in most cases, the problem is that a good bond never developed from the start. For six months, each side has waited for things to improve or has pretended that everything is O.K. Then there's a loss of patience, and both sides are ready to call it quits.

Working to establish a good bond and, if things still go wrong, seeking outside help are probably the best antidotes to this situation.

By contrast, when things are going well for a host family and their student, a delightful chain reaction can be set in motion. It most often begins in mid-January when students have shed the burden of the holiday blues and have begun to enjoy a rekindling of their enthusiasm and warmth—or at least are settling back into normal routines after the holiday excitement. Feeling more inwardly secure, they typically experience a marked improvement in their language skills, which in turn increases their capacity to share their feelings and thoughts. They come alive, radiating both depth and vitality and begin to be more interesting, more three-dimensional, more understandable and more responsive as "friends."

Then as February or March roll around, the family may become acutely aware of how fast time is passing and experience a desire to deepen the relationship as much as possible. A turning point is reached, and there is an urgency to take advantage of all that can be learned and enjoyed. As one host mother states:

> It hits you that the experience is half over; in a few short months a plane will be lifting off with your exchange student in it!
> Suddenly, there's hardly any time left, and there's so much you want to learn about this person. So with the clock ticking, you begin to make every minute count.

To capitalize on the time remaining, special outings to historical sites might be planned, frequent trips made to the library to explore aspects of the student's culture, or Saturdays spent in the kitchen learning how to cook the student's way. At times, the dinner hour may extend late into the evening because your student has developed a knack for sparking lively discussions about cultural differences, U.S. lifestyles or some controversial topic. For some students and families, this phase of the homestay is a time of serious introspection, growing pains and heightened cultural self-awareness.

It is also not uncommon during these last months for students to seek their hosts' opinions and recommendations about matters that pertain to life back home. Confidential talks can develop about such things as mixed feelings for a girl or boy friend, disagreements with natural parents, doubts about one's identity and values, or uncertainties regarding a career direction. In these discussions, the host (who serves as an adult friend to the student) can provide unique help which is not usually available from the adolescent's peers.

One host mother explains that she and her exchange student frequently took advantage of the late night hours, holding long talks between 11 and 3 a.m. "That's when it was quiet, everyone's guard was down, and we could talk freely," she confided. One such evening, her German student wandered in and began talking about his life at home. The mother describes what happened:

> I was curious to learn about Ulrich's family background, but when he told me he had no curfew at home and frequently rode the train alone across Europe, I didn't believe him. I thought: "He's just trying to persuade me to let up on our rules." Then I thought: "Maybe he has that freedom in Germany, but it's certainly a sign that his parents are weird." My next thought was: "Ulrich's freedom is probably very limited. He probably has no curfew on weekends and can ride only certain safe trains."

You might notice a parallel between this mother's experience and that of Axel described in Chapter 2. You'll recall that Axel couldn't believe that in the U.S. boys are not allowed to visit girls in their bedrooms. Before he could accept this difference between the two cultures, Axel went through a series of reactions very similar to that of Ulrich's host mother. Initially, she denied what she had heard, thought her exchange student was trying to manipulate her, surmised that his parents were "weird," and concluded that he was only telling her half-truths.

But the mother decided to delve deeper. She recognized that at one level, she held a set of rules about unsupervised travel and curfews that differed from rules which were enforced by her student's parents in Germany. At another level, she and her student were talking about behaviors and attitudes that were different because they were based on two distinct cultural approaches to life. Here is what the mother thought to herself:

It's my belief that teenagers need to be in bed early on week nights so they'll be rested for school. This means that we as parents have to set a curfew for them.

Ulrich has just told me his German parents know that he will want to get adequate rest and will therefore get to bed at a reasonable time without a curfew. If he'd told me this three months ago, I wouldn't have believed him. But now I trust him and respect what he says. You know, I'm beginning to realize that there's a big difference in our two families' definitions of responsibility. We Americans put responsibility in the parents' hands; German parents give more responsibility to their children.

Another reason I set a curfew for our kids seems to stem from my belief that teenagers who stay out late are up to no good; the boys are raising hell and the girls are getting into trouble with sex. In the U.S., kids are taught that wholesome weekend socializing ends about midnight.

But Ulrich has pointed out that in Germany, it is customary on weekends for teenagers to be out after midnight sitting in cafes drinking beer, dancing and talking philosophy. It seems that teenagers socialize at different times and in different ways in the two cultures.

Regarding travel, I would never permit our teenage son to ride a train alone across the U.S. I don't think it's safe. Besides, it's just not done here.

Now I understand that trains in Europe are sleek and safe. Everyone rides them. My student says that asking a German to avoid trains would be like asking an American to stay away from cars and freeways. Besides, he says Germans believe in "wanderlust"; they believe that travel is important—it has the power to educate young minds.

After exploring these issues, both the student and the host mother had a better understanding of why teenagers are supervised in different ways in the two cultures. Of course, the mother still expected Ulrich to follow the rules for teenagers in her household, but she had a new appreciation for cultural differences and why her student couldn't automatically fit into her family's way of functioning. She could also better understand why long talks and serious discussions were necessary to develop an appreciation for another way of life. What's more, the host mother began to recognize some of her cultural blind spots and cultural innocence. As the mother stated about their session in intercultural learning:

> I realized I wasn't initially able to believe Ulrich because I'd been looking at German behavior with American eyes; I was trapped in my Americanization. To understand Ulrich, I had to see things through his eyes. When I made that shift, I realized, "Gee, it really *is* very different somewhere else!"

What this mother was eventually able to do illustrates what cultural learning is all about: being able to accept your own biases, then suspending them in order to take up residence in another person's point of view. During the culture learning stage, biases and disbelief generally give way to respect, deeper understanding and a blooming international friendship.

To reap the rewards of culture learning, you may want to acquire some cross-cultural communication skills. Described below are some of our ideas and suggestions on how to proceed.

Experienced host families say that discussing cultural differences with an exchange student means communicating in a way that's entirely new. It's not like debating political issues with a friend, selling a new idea to one's boss, explaining abstract concepts to a child or clearing up some misunderstanding with your spouse. Talks with an exchange student about cultural differences means doing things we rarely do in daily conversations: 1) delving into cultural blind spots to examine biases, hidden cultural assumptions and unspoken family rules; 2) clarifying definitions which may be based on cultural factors; 3) putting aside our usual American way of speaking (which is often characterized by hard-hitting factual statements and persuasive arguments); and 4) adopting a more tentative approach and empathic attitude.

Families who have developed an appreciation for other points of view have acquired expertise in what is called intercultural communication. This special cross-cultural fluency is something that family members acquire as they learn about the influence of enculturation, adopt a more empathic way of interacting and gain experience from hosting exchange students.

Over the past few years, the field of intercultural learning and communication has grown substantially, and a variety of books and articles are readily available. A suggested reading list is provided in Appendix A. Occasionally, the sponsoring exchange organizations have printed materials available on these topics.

From your reading, you may discover a number of ideas which you can use to enhance intercultural discussions with your student. You might also try using the following formula:

a. In situations where the student's behavior or comments are confusing, first identify what exactly occurred (the actual words or objective event).

b. Ask yourself what conclusions you are drawing that might reflect your own cultural values, assumptions and perceptions (observer's interpretations/conclusions).

c. Next, discuss the situation with the student, describing the observed event and your interpretations/conclusions.

d. Ask the student to identify what cultural assumptions may have prompted the behavior that you found confusing.

e. As much as possible, put aside your own point of view so that you can see things from your student's perspective.

f. Compare your interpretations/conclusions with the student's assumptions to reach an understanding of what exactly is defined differently in the two cultures.

As host families develop the capacity to see events through both their students' eyes and their own, an appreciation for different cultural patterns is developed. In time, the family and student may each be able to say:

I can understand why you think and feel the way you do. In your country, your behavior and customs are just as logical and appropriate as mine. As they say in Brazil, "O que é diferente não é obrigatoriamente errado"—What is different is not necessarily wrong.

14. Stage Seven: Pre-Departure

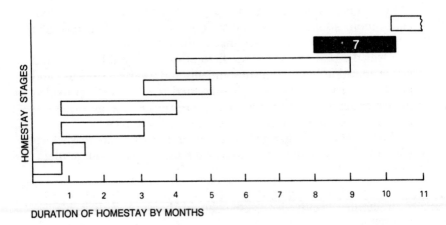

DURATION OF HOMESTAY BY MONTHS

Stage Seven begins near the end of the homestay experience, approximately six weeks prior to the student's departure, and ends when the student leaves.

Sometimes families recoil at the very mention of the term "pre-departure." "The word has a stigma," says one host mother. "To most families it's nothing more than just a nice word for the awful doom and gloom of goodbye."

Although sadness and agitation are often a feature of this period, our view of the pre-departure stage is not, on the whole, negative. On the contrary, we think of the final weeks of the homestay experience as a time to put a good ending to an overall rewarding experience.

The ways that host families and students experience this last stage vary dramatically. In many cases, a closeness develops and special efforts are made to get the most out of the final weeks. In other cases, there is a loosening of the lifestyle sharing bond, resulting in a noticeable shift away from the coziness which characterized relationships in the previous period.

In the latter case, what often begins to surface is discomfort, irritability, hypersensitivity, tension and defensiveness. "Your student begins to break all the rules, acting like a brat with a double-digit IQ," quips one host father. "Rightly or wrongly, you get the feeling of being ignored, as though you've been tossed out like

yesterday's newspaper and your home is being used as a hotel."
Adding to these sentiments, another host parent remarks:

> Things start to go to pot. Everyone starts bellyaching and nit-picking.
> One minute I'm dying to get the experience over and done with, so I
> try driving a mean wedge of anger between myself and our student.
> It's easy to do if I can convince myself I've been used and abused.
> "Good riddance," I broadcast to everyone.
>
> The next minute I'll be the complete opposite: possessive and jealous
> and ashamed about ever thinking of booting him out the door, coaxing
> him to stay forever and saying, "Everyone knows the stork made a
> mistake—he delivered you to the wrong place! You were always meant
> to be *our* kid."

About this same time, families receive in the mail official noti-
fication of the return flight schedule. "I glance at the letter but I
don't pay any attention to it," reveals one mother who reacts to the
news as an unwelcome aggravation:

> When the organization sends that letter, I think, "Why are they
> throwing cold water on our fantastic experience? Why did they send
> this information so early?"
>
> I worry that if I start thinking about the end I'll spend the last two
> months dragging around and feeling crummy. So I just stuff the letter
> in a cluttered drawer and tell myself that there'll be plenty of time to
> deal with the end when the end is here.

Some families find that they can effectively push aside the unpleasant news of their student's imminent departure and continue
coasting through the experience. But many families have learned
that the denial approach can create real heartaches, as another host
mother explains:

> Some families put off talking until their student's flight ticket arrives
> in July. That's a big mistake. By then the days have gotten too frantic
> and nerves too jangled to say the thoughtful things you really want to
> say.
>
> You'd think the last day would be the right time to say all the things
> you've been saving up for months, but it's not. The last day is pure
> madness—crammed with errands, friends popping in and last minute
> packing. Wearily you pile into the car and rush to the airport. "At last,"
> you sigh, "there's time to talk." But there you are, standing in a crowded
> room of strangers, and you find you can't get the words out. So you
> stare at each other, awkwardly shake hands and repeat worn, hollow
> phrases like, "Have a safe trip."

As the plane disappears, you console yourself with the thought, "I'll say everything in a letter." But you know you can't. How can you punctuate a sentence with intimate eye contact or a tender hug?

So the plane flies away, and you're left feeling strangely cheated. "Maria changed our lives so much," you whisper. "Why didn't I take the time to tell her?"

To avoid the situation described above, it's a good idea to begin actively preparing for your student's departure. Because that task may be an unfamiliar one, here are some ways you can proceed:

1. RECOGNIZE FEELINGS

The "goodbye" process begins when the family starts seriously examining their own thoughts and feelings about the impending departure. There may be a variety of reactions: irritation, relief, sadness, confusion, accomplishment, nervousness or a jumbled mixture of all of these.

2. ACCEPT FEELINGS OF LOSS

Frequently, family members find themselves vacillating between feelings of loss and gain. While they recognize that a solid friendship has been established (one that will endure despite separation), they also realize that when their student leaves, the experience of lifestyle sharing will end forever. Another host mother reflects on the bittersweet aspect of this period:

As the days evaporate, you're going to hurt, and you'll be convinced that you, not your student, are the one losing the most. Some days will be great, filled with celebration and tender remembrances; others will be just awful.

You'll fret that once you've parted, the caring will stop, and you'll have a gnawing awareness that something will never be quite the same ever again. Through it all, you may be changed for the better: You may learn that it's O.K. to hurt deeply when you love.

3. LETTING GO

One host father likens saying goodbye to the experience of giving one's daughter away in marriage. In both cases, you're breaking one bond and sanctioning another. "It's not easy to do," the host father admits. "But for the new marriage to work, the parent has to step down and assume a secondary role."

In much the same way, you'll need to relinquish your role as a host parent and return responsibility to your student's natural parents. This can be done by conveying to your student your recognition that he belongs with his natural family (even though in some ways, he may feel better understood by your family), and that he will soon again be involved in their lives. Through such messages, you will, in a very important way, be giving your student permission to return home.

4. TAKE STOCK OF THE HOMESTAY EXPERIENCE

During your final weeks together, it's important to spend some time reviewing the year's experience. "We began scheduling informal evening talks," explains one host father, who said to his student: "Pier, we only have a few brief weeks left together, so let's talk about what it's been like—both the good and the bad moments. Let's explore what we've learned from the experience of living together."

As a part of this review, some families find it helpful to put together two identical scrapbooks of their shared experiences (one for the family to keep and one for the student to take). As photos and keepsakes are assembled, family members have a chance to share personal reactions, talk about what they've learned and describe how they've changed. "It's really heartwarming to see tears in your student's eyes as he tells you this has been the best year of his life," reveals one host mother. Or, as another host mother reports, "All of a sudden I realized that our own daughter had gained two years' maturity during the six months our exchange student was with us. That felt good."

To top off the review, many families plan ways to celebrate their sense of accomplishment, success and growth. Some arrange a special dinner; others give a party or share a quiet weekend together at a camp retreat.

5. PREPARE YOUR STUDENT FOR REVERSE CULTURE SHOCK

It has been said that teenage exchange students travel to not one but two foreign cultures: the one they are visiting and the one they return to. What this means is the somewhat ironic notion that upon returning home, exchange students often find their own home culture strange and even forbidding.

As the departure date approaches, many students fluctuate between feeling quite jubilant and suffering pangs of apprehension. Help can be provided by encouraging your student to discuss his concerns openly. One host mother explains to her students that it is normal for them to feel anxious about returning home. Then she helps them anticipate some of the issues they might face by saying things like:

> You know, your family will certainly notice that you've grown two inches taller, but they may not notice your growth in maturity. What will it be like for you if they don't recognize the inner changes and continue treating you exactly the same? If this becomes a problem for you, how can you help your parents begin to appreciate the ways you've changed? And if that doesn't work, what might you do next?

Other issues related to reverse culture shock that can be discussed include: 1) the possibility of being criticized for appearing "Americanized";[1] 2) feeling out of step with the changes that have taken place at home; 3) feeling awkward speaking one's native language again; 4) being ignored by old friends; 5) missing one's host family; 6) noticing the indifference most people at home will display toward one's international experience; 7) facing school exams; and 8) finding ways to integrate what has been learned into one's daily life.

While discussing these issues will not necessarily produce fail-safe solutions or totally immunize your student against reverse culture shock, it will hopefully reduce the number of unexpected jolts that are encountered. In addition, it may give him a feeling of confidence and optimism that he can deal with what lies ahead.

6. THE FAREWELL

"Saying that final goodbye is never easy," explains a father who over the years has hosted a dozen or more exchange students. "No matter how thoroughly we review what's been gained, no matter how much we communicate to a student that the experience has been exceedingly special and rewarding, those last few hours are filled with intense emotion that words alone cannot adequately express."

In order to express symbolically what words alone cannot, some families give their student a farewell gift on the last day—perhaps a locket, a hand-knit sweater or a framed family photo. One family has developed the custom of giving their student a symbolic house-key on which they inscribe a special message. Another family prepares a thoughtful letter and quietly slips it into their student's pocket before he boards the plane.

Sometimes students also say a special farewell by leaving behind a gift for the household or a hidden note to be discovered at some

later date. One student left an expression of affection which she
had penned on a sliver of cardboard and tacked to a closet door:

> I'd like the memory
> Of me
> To be a happy one.
>
> I'd like to leave
> An afterglow
> Of smiles.
>
> When days are gone,
> I'd like to leave
> An echo
> Whispering softly
> Down the ways,
> Of happy times
> And laughing times.
>
> I'd like the tears
> Of those who grieve
> To dry before the sun,
> As happy memories
> Linger on
> When days are gone.

15. Stage Eight: Re-Adjustment

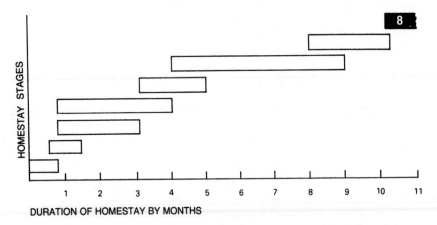

DURATION OF HOMESTAY BY MONTHS

Stage Eight begins with the exchange student's departure and usually continues for three to six weeks. In some subtle ways, this stage may continue for several months as the experience of hosting continues to influence the lives of family members.

"The hosting experience does not come to an end when you say goodbye," states a seasoned host mother. "You don't just drive home from the airport and resume your normal life. There are feelings to be acknowledged, new routines to be considered and a relationship with your former exchange student which will need defining. All this takes time and work."

The ride home from the airport can itself be unsettling. Along with feelings of sadness, there's often a sensation of disbelief, an eerie numbness that gets expressed in the thought, "This isn't really happening, is it? Tomorrow our student will be back and everything will be fine again." One host father described the airport departure this way:

> The ride home—it took forever. In the car, it was cold and quiet, like there had been a death in the family. Everybody was shaken by the emptiness, and everyone was crying a little bit. I didn't totally believe it, but I knew Heidi was gone. And I wondered if I would ever, ever see her again.

Families often experience a period of mourning which may continue for several days or weeks. One person might appear sad and uncommunicative, while others might abound with nervous energy and worried thoughts like, "Oh, I do hope Michio made her connecting flight in San Francisco," or "Sverrir must be back in Iceland now. I wonder if his girl friend came to the airport to meet him. What if he's laughed at for speaking with an American accent?"

A mother who has hosted 15 students explains that the grieving process often centers around her former student's bedroom:

> For the first couple of weeks, I just avoided Jarl's bedroom. Only gradually did I feel strong enough to open the door and walk by. Then one day I went inside. I could hear his voice, and I just stood there and cried.

Another host mother states that she agonized for the first few weeks, having received no communication from her Middle Eastern student. "I became worried and anxious," she says, "thinking that maybe Hatam had fallen off the edge of the earth, or worse, maybe he had stopped caring for us." She describes her family's reactions this way:

> We had this intense longing because a part of our life was missing. Everywhere we looked we found emptiness—a bedroom was empty, a chair at the dinnertable, a shelf in the bathroom cabinet. Everywhere was the message: We've shrunk to one less.

A month after their student has left, most families find that they are beginning to return to normal. Generally, they are able to resume their routines, re-establish comfortable schedules and interact as a family without intense feelings of loss. "You begin to realize that life will go on, and that you can enjoy being a smaller family again," notes one father.

Just when things start to settle down, however, the mailcarrier may deliver the first letter from your former exchange student and again you might feel the turmoil. One mother puts it this way:

> Every day we waited for the mail, so we were ecstatic when an overseas letter finally arrived from Evy. But the message brought us down again because Evy wrote that she was lonely and unhappy and homesick for our family and life in the U.S.

With the hope of providing Evy with some soothing reassurance and insightful guidance, the mother began writing a lengthy response. But as she wrote page after page of advice, she began to realize the limitations of a letter. "It's not the same as a person-to-person dialogue," she explains. "And it hit me that by the time Evy got my response, she would probably have these problems solved and be dealing with new concerns."

Another mother experienced different frustrations with letter writing. She began mailing letters on a weekly basis but received only infrequent responses from her former exchange student. At first she felt annoyed and rejected by the student's "indifference" until she realized her motivations for writing were suspect. She was trying to sustain the relationship at a level which was no longer possible. She explains:

> I wrote Francisco every week because I wanted to keep him abreast of all the family's activities and experiences. I wanted to keep him involved in our lifestyle, but I think he was put off by my frenzied efforts. You see, I didn't want to accept the fact that we were no longer host parents sharing our home and way of life with him.

What both of these mothers came to realize through the experience of letter writing was the practical meaning of saying goodbye. Although each had seen her exchange student board the plane, neither recognized the finality of that departure until she could no longer talk to her student about new ideas and feelings, offer timely advice or share life experiences.

Eventually, both mothers were able to accept the fact that the old way of relating no longer worked. In place of the hosting relationship, they began to enjoy a kind of pen-pal friendship, a friendship not unlike the lingering bond one often cherishes with an old college classmate or a childhood buddy. When this new arrangement was accepted, each family became comfortable with the idea of receiving one or two letters a year from their special overseas friend and perhaps getting a call or photo as a Christmas treat.[1]

Just as parents often find that defining their relationship with a newly-married son or daughter may take time, you might discover that it takes several months and deliberate effort to establish a sort of amiable but distant "absentee friendship" with your former exchange student. "It's not easy," acknowledges one host father, "but once you can let go of needing the relationship to continue, you can begin to savor the experience you had." He discovered that:

> A part of Adriana left four years ago, but a part of her is ours and will be with us forever. She left a vast storehouse of memories that

keep pouring out day after day, year after year. We find that we continue to use her quirky expressions, we remember events by things she did and said, and we see our mundane routines afresh through her innocence and intensity. Some things about the hosting experience have died, but not our memories. They are beautiful, alive and very special.

Perhaps at Christmas several years from now, you will curl up in a chair and find just the right words to express your appreciation and love to that special young man or woman who once spent an eventful year in your home. And perhaps as you look back and remember, your sentiments will be similar to those of the host mother who wrote:

December 21

Dear Torben,

How we wish you could be here next week to be the best man in Mark's wedding. We know that in your last year of medical school, your life is extraordinarily busy. Nonetheless, as the wedding approaches, we feel your absence strongly. And we remember . . .

We remember how you loved to swim, and how you always carried your bathing suit with you "just in case." We remember how you and Mark argued over who could consume the most ice-cream. And who could forget the way you refused to go home? You just couldn't pack. Almost everything left the country bundled in your arms—coats, posters, clothes, souvenirs, you name it. And we remember when you brought your bride, Kirsten, for a visit. We were all ecstatic.

The memories: They go on and on . . .

We still miss you, even after seven years! We learned so much from having you. We learned about you and Denmark, of course. But we also learned so much about ourselves, our family and the United States. Best of all, we learned how people grow—and grow up. Some of that learning is still in progress for us. Maybe it will never end! Maybe growth is like the glistening beam of a flashlight that expands ever outward into the night.

Torben, we will miss you on the 27th, but in another way you will be with us, all day. We send you so much love, and our thanks for all you have given us. There is still a bond, and there always will be. Hurry back!

Much love,

Mary

Postscript: Special Concerns

A few host families will find themselves having to deal with concerns that are a bit out of the ordinary. Just in case it might happen to you, we've included information about exchange students who arrive with special needs and exchange students who are moved to second or third host families. You will also find some guidelines to help you determine whether a sponsoring exchange organization is reputable.

1. STUDENTS WITH SPECIAL NEEDS

Because being an exchange student means having to contend with both the upheavals of adolescence and the stress of cross-cultural adjustment, it could be argued that all teenage sojourners are vulnerable and need considerable guidance and support from a well-prepared host family. In addition, some teenage exchange students arrive with other liabilities that increase their vulnerability and are considered "at-risk." The following are examples:

The Runaway. This is a student who comes from a family that is experiencing a great deal of stress, usually due to marital discord or a recent divorce. The student tries to run away from the unpleasant home situation by becoming an exchange student. Or the natural parents may send the youngster away, believing (naively) that a cross-cultural experience will serve as a pleasant respite. The student often arrives with romanticized expectations, frequently remains preoccupied with the natural family's problems, often experiences rather severe culture shock reactions and may resist the idea of returning home.

The Boarding School Student. This student has spent many years in preparatory schools and is not accustomed to living full-time with a family. She or he may be particularly uncomfortable around young children, have difficulty adjusting to household routines, shy away from family-oriented activities, find it stressful accommodating to a public school and display a reluctance to form close attachments.

The Political Refugee. This student has become an exchange student in order to flee political unrest and perhaps civil war at home. The student's parents might also see the homestay as a means for their child to obtain political asylum in the U.S. Unfortunately, this type of student may have little motivation to participate in family life and may not want to return home. The good news is that not many students of this kind enter into exchange student programs. *Love Affair Refugee.* Students who fit this profile have become exchange students under duress. Their parents decided that a love affair got too intense and the couple should be separated for a while. This student may have great difficulty making new friends, feel quite a bit of resentment and experience some intense bouts of homesickness.

Students who arrive with one of the foregoing concerns often have a more difficult adjustment, and it is sometimes best if they are placed with an experienced host family that is prepared to handle special problems. If the student you are hosting falls into one of the "at-risk" categories (it has been estimated that perhaps one out of every five students do), we recommend that you contact the sponsoring student exchange program.

2. RE-PLACEMENTS TO SECOND AND THIRD HOST FAMILIES

Although the majority of homestay experiences are successful, there are cases in which the initial placement doesn't work out and the exchange student must be moved to one or more other host families. What little research there is indicates that 25% to 30% of initial host families will not keep their student for the entire home-stay experience.

While it may be unpleasant to think about losing a student, knowing that changes do occur with some frequency can help ease any possible feelings of failure. Also, knowing how to cope successfully with a replacement situation can reduce the stress experienced by both the student and the family.

Why do some placements fail? There is no single reason. And because the phenomenon has not been thoroughly researched, it is not easy to predict which factors promote success and which lead to failure.[1] One study, however, has looked at the sojourner's role in successful overseas experiences and has identified the following three characteristics: realistic but positive pre-arrival expectations, effective interpersonal skills and a solid sense of personal identity.[2]

Described below are the most common reasons that homestay experiences become unsatisfactory:

A Poor Match. Sometimes differences in lifestyle, interests and/

or personalities are so great that accommodation is impossible for either the student, the host family or both.[3]

At-Risk Students. When vulnerable students are placed with host families that are not prepared to handle their special needs, the experience can become a burden on the family; a second home will then be sought for the student.

Communication Breakdowns. Various factors can predispose a family and student to communication problems: tendency to be indirect or vague when speaking, a rigid right-wrong mentality, low tolerance for stress and ambiguity, and a tendency to deny or ignore problems when they arise.

When misunderstandings (cross-cultural or otherwise) are not resolved as they occur, an atmosphere of distrust and defensiveness can develop. Sometimes conflict and misunderstanding grow so intense that problem-solving is hampered. Then the best solution may be for the student to move.

Antagonism Within the Family. This can occur if the preferential treatment given to the exchange student borders on favoritism, causing the host children to feel ignored and resentful. In addition, conflict can develop between the student and a sibling if either of them occasionally assumes the role of a parental substitute who disciplines or dictates to the other.[4]

Extenuating Circumstances. There are instances when a host family's situation changes in such a way that they are precluded from keeping the student. This can happen when such things as illness in the family, loss of employment or relocation occur.

Unmet Expectations. Sometimes a family will enter the hosting experience with unrealistic expectations. Lacking an awareness of the financial outlay, the adaptation required or the amount of learning involved, some families become disenchanted and choose to end the experience.

When it becomes necessary for a student to move to a second host family,[5] the transition can be eased if the reasons for leaving are openly discussed and blame is avoided. Everyone may feel relieved when the transition is completed, but it is important to bear in mind that saying goodbye may be painful for everybody involved. Frequently, families as well as students feel sad, guilty and rejected for a period of time. After the student's departure, it is important for family members to evaluate the experience as a whole by identifying what was learned as well as what mistakes were made.

Some sponsoring organizations do not encourage families to contact students once they have moved. However, other organizations encourage continued contact. In those cases, the friendship that developed can continue.

3. UNRESPONSIVE SPONSORING ORGANIZATIONS

There are federal regulations[6] for teenage exchange organizations (which are outlined in Appendix B), but only those programs which apply for a government designation number are bound by the regulations. As a result, the quality and kinds of services offered by the exchange programs vary widely. In addition, no one knows exactly how many programs exist or how many foreign students arrive in the U.S. in a given year. A rough estimate is that somewhere between 50 and 100 programs are currently in operation. Estimates for the annual number of exchangees vary between 10,000 and 300,000.

Although families and students give some organizations high marks for the quality of their services, others are felt to be quite poorly administered. For example, one of the more prestigious programs reports that at one time, as many as 15% of its foreign students did not have host families upon arrival.[7] And, for some programs, as many as one student in ten has to return to his or her home country prematurely because of an inability to adjust, rule violations or at-home emergencies. This 10% early return rate raises questions about the effectiveness of selection procedures (for students and hosts), the quality of support services and the helpfulness of local representatives.

Sometimes an enraged host family will come across a particularly shoddy program and bombard Congress and embassies with allegations that a few of the student exchange organizations seem to be little more than "meat markets" which go into countries and recruit kids for a price. In one school district, teachers and administrators complained that in some programs the only criteria for accepting students was that they had the "bucks to pay for it." In these cases, the students came with no English, they were provided little or no orientation, school officials felt pressured and manipulated by the sponsoring organizations, and students were placed with any family who said they'd take one. Explained one irate official: "For the school and kid, it was just a lost nine months."[8]

In recent years, both the number of students involved in exchanges and the number of exchange programs have increased dramatically. Not surprisingly, this rapid growth has been paralleled by a dramatic increase in the number of complaints against the programs. As a result, some school boards are refusing to enroll exchange students from certain programs, other school districts have imposed standards on programs and a few officials are going so far as to refer to adolescent homestay programs as the "Teenage International Ill-will Phenomenon."

In the spring of 1983, the National Association of Secondary School Principals (NASSP) conducted a fact-finding study to ascertain how high school principals rated the various teenage exchange programs. Responses from 850 schools in all 50 states revealed that over a three-year period roughly half the schools had received complaints about programs from either teachers, host families or students. In general, most schools evaluated the concept of student exchange as positive, but John Kourmadas, assistant to the NASSP executive director, said that the complaint rate was high enough to suggest that most of the exchange programs needed to take corrective action. Kourmadas also emphasized that the complaint rate tended to be closely related to the effectiveness of each program's local representatives. When local personnel functioned well, complaints tended to be low; when they did not, the complaint rate went up. He urged prospective host families to check with school officials and seasoned host families for their ratings of local exchange organization representatives before becoming involved with a program regardless of the program's national reputation.[9]

Because these concerns are being raised, we think it is important for you to know how to identify a quality program. Listed below are some questions you might want to ask. If your answers are "yes," then we think the organization probably deserves a high rating. On the other hand, if you have more "no" answers than you are comfortable with, you might refer to Appendix D of this book for a list of organizations which handle information and complaints about exchange programs.

1. Is the organization willing to provide you with a realistic picture of the hosting experience so that you have an idea not only of the attractions but also of the drawbacks involved?

2. Does the organization have a policy of bringing foreign students to the U.S. only when permanent homes have been pre-arranged? If the policy exists, is it followed consistently?

3. Are families and students carefully screened prior to selection?

4. Is orientation provided for both the student and the host family?

5. Are services (such as assistance from field representatives, a handbook of program policies, counseling sessions, reading materials) made available to students and families?

6. Does the organization provide complete health and accident insurance (or comparable coverage) for the student?

7. Does the organization guarantee air fare if the student wants or needs to return home before the end of the program? If so, is the ticket available to the student without unnecessary delays?

APPENDICES

Appendix A
Suggested Reading List

EDUCATIONAL SYSTEMS

1. Kohls, L. Robert. "The Conflict between Islamic and Western Values in the Classroom," in *Developing Intercultural Awareness*. Washington D.C.: The Society for Intercultural Education, Training, and Research, 1981, pp. 23–26. (Also available from the Intercultural Press, Yarmouth, Maine.)

Thuy, Vuong, G. "Learning Style and Teaching Approach," in *Getting to Know the Vietnamese and Their Culture*. New York: Frederick Ungar Publishing Company, 1976, pp. 71–82.

CULTURE SHOCK

Craig, JoAnn, "Culture Shock: The Mysterious Malady," in *Culture Shock*. Singapore: Times Books International, 1979.

INTERCULTURAL LEARNING

Batchelder, D. "The Green Banana," in *Beyond Experience: The Experimental Approach to Cross-cultural Education*. Donald Batchelder and Elizabeth Warner (Eds.), Brattleboro, Vermont: The Experiment Press, 1977, pp. 137–140.

Condon, John, & Yousef, Fathi. *An Introduction to Intercultural Communication*. New York: Bobbs-Merrill, 1975. (Also available from Intercultural Press, Yarmouth, Maine.)

Fersh, Seymour. *Learning About Peoples and Cultures*. Evanston, Ill.: McDougal & Littell, 1974.

Fieg, John P. & Blair, John G. *There Is a Difference: 17 Intercultural Perspectives*. Washington, D.C.: Meridian House International, 1980.

Hall, Edward. *The Silent Language*. Garden City, New York: Anchor Press, 1959.

Kohls, L. Robert. *Survival Kit for Overseas Living*. Yarmouth, Maine: Intercultural Press, 1984.

Samovar, Larry & Porter, Richard (Eds.). *Intercultural Communication: A Reader*. Belmont, California: Wadsworth, 1976.

Smith, Elise & Luce, Louise Fiber (Eds.). *Toward Internationalism*. Rowley, Mass.: Newbury House, 1979. (Also available from Intercultural Press, Yarmouth, Maine.)

LANGUAGE LEARNING

Rubin, Joan and Thompson, Irene. *How to Be a More Successful Language Learner*. Boston: Heinle & Heinle, 1982. (Also available from Intercultural Press, Yarmouth, Maine.)

LIFESTYLES

Feldman, Saul & Theilbar, Gerald (Eds.). *Lifestyles: Diversity in American Society*. Boston: Little, Brown, and Company, 1975.

Johnson, Sheila K. "Sociology of Christmas Cards," in *Lifestyles: Diversity in American Society*. Boston: Little, Brown, and Company, 1975, pp. 177–182.

Mitchell, Arnold. *The Nine American Lifestyles: Who We Are, Where We Are Going*. New York: MacMillan, 1983.

GENERAL

Brown, Ina Corinne. *Understanding Other Cultures*. Inglewood Cliffs, New Jersey: Prentice-Hall, 1963.

Hazelline, Mary. *Anniversaries and Holidays: A Calendar of Days and How to Celebrate Them*. Washington, D.C.: American Library Association, 1969.

STUDENT SOJOURNS

Beals, R. & Humphrey, N. *No Frontier to Learning: The Mexican Student in the United States*. Minneapolis: University of Minnesota Press, 1957.

Gorden, Raymond. *Living in Latin America*. Skokie, Illinois: National Textbook Company, 1974. (Also available from the Intercultural Press, Yarmouth, Maine.)

Hull, III, W. Frank. *Foreign Students in the United States of America*. New York: Praeger, 1978.

Useem, John & Useem, Ruth. *The Western Educated Man in India*. New York: Dryden, 1955.

U.S. CULTURE

Bellah, Robert. "Civil Religion in America," in *Lifestyles: Diversity in American Society*. Saul Feldman and Gerald Thielbar, (Eds.), Boston: Little, Brown, and Company, 1975, pp. 16–33.

Berger, Bennett. "On the Youthfulness of Youth Cultures," in *Lifestyles: Diversity in American Society*. Saul Feldman and Gerald Thielbar, (Eds.), Boston: Little, Brown, and Company, 1975, pp. 298–320.

Bouraoui, H. A. "Living Next Door to an Elephant: Canadian Reactions to the American Ethos," in *Lifestyles: Diversity in American Society*. Saul Feldman and Gerald Thielbar, (Eds.), Boston: Little, Brown, and Company, 1975, pp. 45–58.

Inge, M. Thomas, (Ed.). *Handbook of American Popular Culture*. Westport, Connecticut: Greenwood Press, 1978.

Lanier, Alison. *Living in the U.S.A.* Yarmouth, Maine: Intercultural Press, 1981.

Stewart, Edward. *American Cultural Patterns: A Cross-cultural Perspective*. Yarmouth, Maine: Intercultural Press, 1971.

Appendix B
United States Information Agency Guidelines for Teenage Exchange Programs

Programs that receive student J-Visa documentation through the government are expected to adhere to the guidelines that have been established by the United States Information Agency (USIA), Bureau of Educational and Cultural Affairs, Teenage Exchange Visitor Office. Periodically, the USIA guidelines are updated and revisions can be obtained by writing directly to the Exchange Visitor Office in Washington, D.C. (see Appendix D for the address and telephone number).

The regulations that were in effect when this book was published appeared in the Federal Register (Volume 44, Number 59) on March 26, 1979; revisions were printed in Volume 48, Number 214, Nov. 3, 1983. They are briefly summarized in the following paragraph.

1. *Approved Sponsors.* Employment or travel agencies shall not be used for recruitment of foreign students. Also, programs must be run by non-profit organizations.

2. *Applicant's Age.* Selection of participants will be limited to secondary school students between the ages of 15 and 19.,

3. *Applicant's Language Proficiency.* Participants should have sufficient knowledge of English to function in an English speaking environment.

4. *Applicant's Readiness.* Students should be screened for demonstrated maturity and ability to get maximum benefit from the program.

5. *Written Contracts.* All provisions expected by the sponsoring organization should be written (preferably in English and the natural family's native language). The terms should specify the total costs, refund policies, program rules and regulations. Programs are responsible for assuring that these terms are fully understood.

6. *Authorization by School Officials.* Students shall not be considered accepted by the public schools without the prior approval of area school officials. The high school placement should be arranged by the sponsoring organization at least five weeks in advance of the student's arrival in the U.S. Travel should not be arranged for a student unless the student has been accepted (in writing) by the school principal or superintendent where the student will be enrolled.[1] Copies of letters of acceptance should be maintained by the sponsoring organization.

7. *Orientation for Students.* Both pre-departure and arrival orientation must be provided to all students. Orientation should give students basic information about the U.S. and should include full information about the sponsoring organization's policies.

8. *Orientation for Hosts.* Orientation must also be provided to host families in advance of the student's arrival. Each host family should be well briefed on the family and cultural patterns of the foreign student's country. Each family should also be apprised of potential problems in hosting and provided with suggestions on how to cope with normal adjustment problems.

9. *Personal Identification Cards.* Students must be provided with an identification card which includes: 1) the name and phone number of the sponsoring organization, 2) name, address and phone number of the Exchange Visitor Office in Washington, D.C. Host families should also be provided with names of persons they can contact at USIA if outside help is needed.

10. *Information to Families and Students.* The sponsoring organization is expected to provide students and families with a current copy of the USIA guidelines called the "Criteria For Exchange Visitor Teenage Programs."

11. *Medical Insurance.* Sponsors are responsible for seeing that every student has appropriate medical coverage.

12. *Student Employment.* Foreign students are not permitted to accept full-time employment during their stay in the U.S. However, students may take on small neighborhood jobs such as tutoring, baby sitting, newspaper delivery, etc. to earn spending money.

13. *Geographical Distribution of Students.* Every effort should be made to have students widely dispersed throughout the country. No more than four foreign students and no more than two of the same nationality should be placed in one high school by a sponsor.

14. *Selection of Host Families.* A program's representative must personally interview and visit the home of each potential host family. Telephone interviews are not sufficient. Host families should be selected prior to the student's arrival and they should be given background data on the student at least five weeks prior to receiving a foreign student. This provision allows families and students the opportunity to begin getting acquainted through an exchange of letters and phone calls. Non-compliance with this requirement for advance placements can result in suspension or revocation of exchange visitor program designation.

Sponsors must make every effort to assure that students are placed with families which promise the greatest compatibility. In this regard, the host family should have at home during non-school hours at least one family member, preferably a teenager, to assure the exchange student of some companionship.

15. *Support Services Provided by Sponsor.* Host families and students should be contacted periodically by the sponsor to ensure that problems are dealt with promptly and effectively.

16. *Evaluation of Experience.* Sponsors must solicit written evaluations at the termination of the sojourn. Student evaluations should include discussion of host families, schools, area representatives, orientation. Host family evaluations should include evaluations of students, area representatives, and orientation, and suggest improvements.

17. *Guaranteed Return Travel.* The sponsor must guarantee return transportation for students through the use of escrow accounts.

18. *Audited Financial Statements.* Sponsors are required to have available for review by USIA an audited financial statement of their operation. The financial statement should include an itemized list of the salaries of the officers of the organization.

19. *Annual Reports.* Sponsors will furnish USIA with an annual report on their programs at the close of each year.

20. *Suspension or Revocation of Designation.* Sponsors who are found to be in violation of the above criteria are subject to having their designations suspended for 60 days. Before revocation, formal proceedings must be initiated.

Appendix C
Thinking of Hosting an Exchange Student?

If you are interested in hosting an exchange student but have not made a final decision, you may want to know what things you can do to improve your family's chances of becoming involved with a responsible, quality program. To help with that choice, some suggestions are listed below:

1. *Meet with School Officials.* Contact your high school principal or school counselor to get a profile of the organization and to find out whether or not the school accepts students affiliated with it.

2. *Talk with Experienced Families.* Ask experienced host families if they have been satisfied with the program, if the support services were adequate and if promised services were available and helpful.

3. *Find Out the Organization's Reputation.* To obtain information about the kinds of complaints, if any, that have been lodged against particular programs, contact one of the following:

United States Information Agency (USIA)
General Council's Office
Exchange Visitors Facilitative Staff
400 C Street, S.W.
Washington, D.C. 20547
Phone: (202) 485–7962

The Nat'l Assoc. of Secondary School Principals (NASSP)
1904 Association Drive
Reston, Virginia 22091
Phone: (703) 860–0200

The Council of Chief State School Officers (CCSSO)
379 Hall of States
400 N. Capitol St., N.W.
Washington, D.C. 20001
Phone: (202) 624–7702

U.S. Department of Education
Division of International Education
7th & D Streets, S.W.
Washington, D.C. 20202
Phone: (202) 245–9692

4. *Learn About Policies.* From the organization, inquire about the following: the criteria used to select students; the timing of host family placements (should be completed prior to the student's arrival in the U.S.); the schedule of orientation and pre-departure sessions for arriving and departing students respectively; and the kind of routine contact the organization maintains with the student and host family.

5. *Ask About Special Services.* Find out what special services are available to students and families when problems and emergencies arise. Inquire about the following: Is medical insurance provided by the program? Are counseling services available? Is there a hot line number to call? Does the organization maintain a special financial account for emergencies? If so, does the account guarantee travel home if an emergency early return is required? If the student arrives with minimal English, are language classes or tutors provided?

6. *Meet with the Local Representatives.* Since a local representative will be your link to the sponsoring organization and its support services, it is important that the local representative live in your community and be trained to help with normal adjustment concerns. This person should also be someone with whom you feel comfortable but should not be someone who is a best friend or neighbor. Such people may find it difficult to maintain objectivity when consulted for help during the hosting experience. If a friend or neighbor should ask you to take a student, you might agree to the request but ask that a representative from another area of the community be assigned to help you and your student.

7. *Identify the Program's Mission.* Is the emphasis education, travel, adventure, a family living experience or what? Programs that promote travel as their primary goal may not provide orientation or support services.

8. *Evaluate the Promotional Materials.* Is the emphasis placed on fun and adventure without presenting a realistic picture of both stresses and rewards? Does the literature erroneously describe the USIA designation status by referring to it as a special endorsement or "U.S. approved program"? A designation number from USIA is not a stamp of approval and to imply otherwise is misleading.

9. *Learn How Students are Assigned.* It is important to know what steps will be taken to achieve a good match between your family and the student you receive. In addition, you may want to make sure that you will be given

background data and arrival information on the student at least three weeks prior to the date of the student's arrival in the U.S. That way you will have time to make contact and begin the "getting acquainted" process that gets the new relationship off to a good start.

10. *Inquire About Special Services for Hosts.* Are there orientation opportunities and literature to prepare the family and provide practical guidance? Also, you may want to ask if special counseling and support services are provided to families who host at-risk students. (At-risk students are described in the Postscript to this book.)

11. *Ask for the USIA Regulations.* According to the USIA guidelines, host families are to be provided with a copy of the current federal regulations (which are briefly summarized in Appendix B).

12. *Ask for Important Statistics.* It might be valuable for you to request the following statistics: 1) the number of students assigned to your local area representative (when large numbers are assigned, it can be difficult for the representative to take a personal interest in the student or your family's needs); 2) the percentage of students who arrive without preassigned permanent families having been assigned; 3) the percentage of replacements to second and third families (good matches between the student and family cannot easily be predicted and knowing the replacement rate can give you some idea of how high the chances are that a student will remain in your home for the entire homestay experience); 4) the percentage of students who require counseling; 5) the early return rates.

13. *Check the Financial Records.* Many of the organizations state that their financial records are available for audit by responsible parties. You might want to inquire about how the program fee is spent and what the salary range is for executive employees.

14. *Evaluate Programs on Their Own Merits.* As you review each program, don't automatically assume that "for-profit" programs are exploitative or that "non-profit" programs are responsibly run. There are quality programs in both categories.

15. *Inquire About the Costs to the Student.* Because the baseline program fee varies, it is best that you check with individual organizations for prices. Bear in mind that in addition to the program fee, student costs include the money they are expected to bring for personal expenses. It is difficult to give an exact figure on the amount of spending money students need, but it is estimated to be roughly 80% of the program fee for students on 10-month homestays. For those participating in shorter visits (6 weeks to 6 months), the student's personal expenses will be somewhat less (approximately 60% of the program fee).

16. *Inquire About the Costs to the Host Family.* Although European programs frequently pay host families, U.S. programs rarely do. If the pro-

motional materials say that all you have to provide is room, board and love, ask how much this may amount to financially. Many families report that the cost of hosting for the typical 10-month homestay is approximately 80% of the student's program fee. This amount excludes special trips or expensive gifts. For shorter homestays, the cost would be approximately 60% of the program fee.

17. *Clarify Your Reasons for Getting Involved.* When a family takes an exchange student for the wrong reasons or has unrealistic expectations about what the homestay experience will be like, disappointment and failure can result. Discuss your motivations openly and talk to experienced host families to learn if your plans seem realistic. (Expectations are described in Chapter 9.)

18. *Consider Your Family's Current Situation.* Hosting a foreign student can be a rewarding, enjoyable experience. But bear in mind that hosting is also expensive and stressful. If you are planning a move, if there is illness in the family, if a spouse is unemployed or if your marriage is a bit shaky, it may be that now is not the best time to invite an exchange student into your home. Carefully evaluate your family's readiness for the hosting experience so that you maximize the potential for its success.

19. *Give Thought to the Decision.* When you are interviewed by the sponsoring organization, postpone making a final decision until you have all the information you feel you need and until you have had adequate time to think about it.

20. *Avoid Being Pressured.* Sometimes families feel emotionally coerced into a premature decision because they are told a student is here and waiting for a home. Concern for a homeless exchange student is commendable, but it is not a sufficient reason to enter prematurely into a homestay experience. Try to base your decision on healthy motivations that take into consideration what's best for your family.

21. *Insist on Complete Information.* Has the organization asked you to sign a document confirming that you have been provided with complete information? We think such action is advisable. It is important that you have a thorough understanding of what your responsibilities and those of the sponsoring organization will be. As you are probably aware, this is known as informed consent; we think you should have it.

Appendix D
Who To Contact For Help

If you have questions or concerns about some aspect of the hosting experience, the first person you may want to contact is the local representative of the sponsoring exchange organization. If, however, you feel the matter cannot be resolved at the local level or through channels within the sponsoring organization, you may wish to contact one of the following:

1. Your U.S. Senator or Representative in Washington, D.C. (Your local library should have their addresses.)

2. United States Information Agency (USIA)
   General Council's Office
   Exchange Visitor Facilitative Staff
   400 C Street, S.W.
   Washington, D.C. 20547
   Phone: (202) 485–7962
   (This agency regulates all programs that grant J visas to exchange students but does not oversee programs that grant F visas.)

3. House Foreign Affairs Committee
   Subcommittee on International Operations
   B–358 RHOB
   Washington, D.C. 20547
   Phone: (202) 225–3424
   (This congressional subcommittee handles Department of State and USIA operations and legislation, international education and cultural affairs.)

4. Senate Foreign Relations Committee
   Subcommittee on Arms Control, Oceans, International Operations, and Environment
   4229 DSOB
   Washington, D.C. 20547
   Phone: (202) 224–5842

ENDNOTES

Introduction

1. With full knowledge that the Americas include North, Central and South America, we are using the word "American" in this book to refer specifically to the people living in the United States. This usage was chosen because of its vernacular popularity and is done through no lack of appreciation for the many cultures and nationalities that are equally American.

Chapter 1

1. Frequently, host parents will invite their student to address them as "Mom" and "Dad." We see no problem with this as long as the student is comfortable with the arrangement and as long as it is understood that the host family is not assuming a role that will preempt or rival the role of the student's natural parents. For more details, please refer to the section in Chapter 8 entitled, "Decisions about Names."

2. Of course, exchange students are not necessarily sexually active, and we are by no means suggesting that female exchange students should be using birth control. But as a host parent, it is important for you to let your student know that you are available to discuss such matters if the need arises.

Chapter 2

1. The examples described in this book come from real-life situations involving actual exchange students and host families. Names, however, have been changed to insure anonymity.

Chapter 3

1. Raymond Gorden, *Living in Latin America*. Skokie, Illinois: National Textbook Company, 1974.

2. In Eduardo's culture, teenagers socialize with their friends on weekends beginning around 9 p.m. and may not return home until several hours after midnight.

3. Gorden, *Op. cit.*

Chapter 4

1. This term has been popularized by Edward Stewart, author of *American Cultural Patterns: A Cross-cultural Perspective.*

2. "What the World Thinks of America," Newsweek, 102:2, pp. 44-50, July 11, 1983.

Chapter 5

1. Eleonore Evers, "Foreign Teen-aged Exchange Students in America: Relationships with Families, Peers, and Schools." Ph.D. dissertation, Michigan State University, 1979. The majority of the 52 exchangees who completed questionnaires for this study described the homestay as satisfying even though they experienced periods of stress.

2. The Experiment in International Living. *Adjusting to a New Culture: Culture Shock.* Brattleboro, Vermont (undated article).

3. S. Lysgaard, "Adjustment in a Foreign Society: Norwegian Fulbright Grantees Visiting the United States," *International Social Science Bulletin,* 1955, *7*, pp. 45-51. Later the U curve was revised to include reverse culture shock (making it a double U or W curve). J.T. Gullahorn and J.E. Gullahorn, "An Extension of the U-Curve Hypothesis," *Journal of Social Issues,* 1963, *19*(3), pp. 33-47.

4. A.C. Garza-Guerrero, "Culture Shock: Its Mourning and the Vicissitudes of Identity," *Journal of the American Psychoanalytic Association,* 1974, *22*(2), pp. 422-23.

Chapter 7

1. This term applies to adolescent sojourners who arrive with liabilities that increase the risk of failure. For more information, see the Postscript to this book.

Chapter 8

1. We have not described the period before the student's arrival since many families are not recruited very far in advance of the student's arrival. However, when families receive the name of their student several weeks

prior to arrival, an important bonding process can begin through the exchange of letters and phone calls. Through these contacts, both the family and student begin developing realistic expectations of the other. And, equally important, feelings of caring and interest begin to grow.

2. Arrival fatigue is experienced by female exchange students as well. Beginning in this chapter, we will use the male pronoun for general references throughout an entire chapter and then switch to the female pronoun in alternate chapters. This is done to avoid using only the masculine pronoun. But whatever pronoun is used, the example will always apply to both sexes, except for references to specific individuals.

3. Robbins Hopkins, "Defining and Predicting Overseas Effectiveness for Adolescent Exchange Students." Ph.D. dissertation, University of Massachusetts, 1982. This research suggests that successful sojourners have open communication and a close relationship with their natural parents.

4. For suggestions to help with language learning, see Chapter 10 and Appendix A.

5. Many private schools as well as public schools welcome exchange students and often waive tuition. A growing number have organized their own programs in which students and/or faculty are exchanged.

Chapter 9

1. There may be cases when this does not occur or occurs somewhat later than the five-week point, as is documented by Cornelius Grove, Bettina Hansel and Nancy Painter in an in-progress AFS study: "The Dynamics of Hosting," (personal communication, 1983).

Chapter 10

1. Gorden, *Op. cit.* While studying the non-linguistic communication patterns between American exchange students and their Colombian hosts, the researcher found that household rules and expectations were seldom discussed. In addition, of all areas in the home, the bathroom generated the most misunderstanding. After living with a family for six months, most American students had not learned the rules (spoken or unspoken) for appropriate usage of this area of the home. Colombians and Americans each falsely concluded the other was "unclean," "inconsiderate" and "arrogant."

2. Nancy King, "Case Study of a Latin American Sojourner: Crossing Hard Times." Ph.D. dissertation, Wayne State University, 1981. The subject of this study, a Brazilian exchange student, reported that friendship-

making with American youth was hampered by ethnocentrism, ignorance of other cultures, socio-economic differences and teenage subculture barriers. For the most part, he related best to other foreign students during his six-month sojourn. Officials suggest that this case is representative of the friendship patterns of most teenage exchange students.

Chapter 11

1. Caution: Culture shock may appear at a somewhat later period for some students. Also, many will deny that they are going through culture shock no matter how apparent or severe the symptoms. Finally, there are some students who seem to breeze through the entire exchange experience without suffering from culture shock at all—though in some cases this might be attributable either to their skill in hiding symptoms or the failure of others to perceive them. The information in this chapter, therefore, should be applied and adapted according to the experience of your family and your student.

1   2. Cultural identity refers to one's sense of membership in a particular culture and identification with its values and traditions.

Chapter 13

1. Cornelius Grove reports findings from the in-progress AFS "Dynamics of Hosting" study which indicate that some students experience acute difficulty during this period (personal communication, 1983).

Chapter 14

1. Ralph L. Beals and Norman D. Humphrey, *No Frontier to Learning: The Mexican Student in the United States.* Minneapolis: University of Minnesota Press, 1957. In this study, Mexican students attending U.S. universities reported that they felt somewhat defrauded upon returning to Mexico because they did not receive the attention or prestige they expected. Many blamed their estrangement on the United States and became more nationalistic to avoid criticism that they had been "Americanized."

Chapter 15

1. It is also a sad fact that some students do not write after their return home.

Postscript: Special Concerns

1. Aletha White, "A Study of the Teenage Foreign Exchange Program Based on Host Family Changes." M.A. Project, Wayne State University,

1973. Responses from questionnaires completed by 200 former exchange students did not identify factors that predict re-placements. At the time, the re-placement rate was 30% for the sponsoring exchange organization. When evaluating the overall sojourn, students were not influenced by host family changes.

2. Frank Hawes and Daniel Kealey, "An Empirical Study of Canadian Technical Assistance." *International Journal of Intercultural Relations*, 1981, 5, pp. 239-258.

3. Hugh Russell and F. James Seaman, "Preliminary Report on an Evaluation of Youth For Understanding's 1975-76 Foreign Student Exchange Program," 1976. Students reported that major differences between themselves and their hosts were not necessarily cause for concern. However, when discussion of differences—particularly on topics of politics, esthetics and religion—led to continuing disagreements, students were more likely to change families.

4. *Ibid.* This study revealed that antagonism typically occurs between the student and the oldest daughter who is charged on occasion with disciplining her siblings and may assume the same role with the exchange student.

5. If you have received a student who has previously lived with another host family, the adjustment process may be different from the one we describe in this book. We suggest you contact the sponsoring organization if help is needed.

6. To expedite visa documentation, many but not all of the teenage homestay programs apply for an official U.S. Information Agency (USIA) designation number through the Exchange Visitor Program Office. Until recently, guidelines issued by the Program Office were not legally binding. However, the guidelines have of late been upgraded to regulations, giving the Program Office legal authority to require compliance on the part of the designated homestay programs. Nonetheless, at the time this book was published, many of the regulations were not being adhered to by some of the oldest and best-known exchange organizations.

7. The students were temporarily placed with what were sometimes called "Welcoming Families," a euphemism which belied the fact that federal government regulations, to which the program committed itself, were being violated.

8. *Waterloo Courier*, Waterloo, Iowa, Summer, 1976.

9. Other issues that should be considered before deciding to host an exchange student are presented in Appendix C.

Appendix B

1. This stipulation was still under consideration when this book was published.

INDEX